LOVING IS LIVING

Unfulfilled expectations lead to unhappiness

Timeless counsel and wisdom by

Bob Garon

First printing 1979

Published by VGV PUBLICATIONS

Printed in the United States of America.

Cover layout and internal formatting:
Francisca de Zwager

For information: P.O Box MCPO 2099
Sen Gil Puyat Avenue, Makati City, Philippines, 1260
or www.facebook.com/bobgaron

ISBN: 978-1-7378277-3-3

Royalties earned from this book will help poor children in the Philippines get an education.

To the people of the Philippines,
who have loved me and caused me to grow,
I dedicate this book as a sign of
my deepest affection and regard.

Contents

Foreword

It is with deep honor to write the Foreword for "Loving is Living." I only have words of admiration for the Garon family.

I first met Bob around 1966, taking his "Curcillo" with other college students. We knew him as Fr. Bob. Then I met his young wife, Emmy, in the early 80s in the early education circles. Bob and Emmy started their preschools then and so did I. She always spoke of Bob with great love. I became a *ninang* to their older daughter, Vanessa, and saw how she bloomed in her work and love life. I can fully say that the Garons practice what they preach. And it is all in the books Emmy has lovingly republished.

Bob has consistently advocated that being in love with the Lord, with each other, and with others gives more meaning to life (or living) on earth! Love, though, has many meanings and levels, and this is what this book reveals.

Bob has so many admirable qualities that make him a good counselor and writer. Allow me to focus on two regarding how he responds to relational problems.

One, Bob is realistic in addressing difficult or unhappy relationships. I was a faithful reader of his newspaper columns, and each situation he presented was unique; and yet, one could see this situation in more people's lives. Bob's analysis of unhappiness or expectations and his steps to healing are realistic and possible.

Two, Bob's standards are lofty, and if you read his writings, your ideals will become clearer, even elevated. I believe Bob gives the reader choices in life. We have that freedom to choose good from bad, right from wrong. He also refers to the inner thoughts and feelings of those who seek counseling.

I highly recommend these books of Bob to young people to better prepare themselves in the journey of relationships; to parents, who may have some blind spots on raising their kids; and to educators to better understand human relations. His advice is as relevant today as when he first wrote them, for a better tomorrow.

Thank you dear Emmy, Vanessa, and Alexandra for republishing this book, from which I certainly had new learnings.

Nina Lim- Yuson, PhD
Founder & Chair, Museo Pambata Foundation Inc.
National President, Girl Scouts of the Philippines
(Manila, 2024)

Introduction

Why are so many of us unhappy so often? Why all these fed up, discouraged and depressed feelings? What is it that makes us so miserable that we sometimes just want to lie down and die? I have asked myself these same questions countless times. However, I could never seem to find the right answers.

In fact, what I was looking for was THE reason for all unhappiness. I felt that unless I knew the cause of all unhappiness, I would be destined to go right on walking into one unhappy situation after the other.

Then, a few months ago, I stumbled onto one sentence in my readings that seemed to me to summarize why we are unhappy. "All unhappiness," it said, "stems from unfulfilled expectations." These words struck deeply into my brain. Why had I not thought of this before? It is true. All unhappiness can somehow ultimately be traced to unfulfilled expectations. I have tried to find one, just one, situation where an unfulfilled expectation was NOT at the root of my unhappiness. I have been unable to do so. Every single unhappy moment in my life can be seen as some form of unfulfilled expectation.

I believe this to be a universal truth that can easily be perceived by all men. A woman loses her husband. She is unhappy because she expected him to live longer, but he died. A teenager is unhappy because he expected his love to work out, but it didn't. A worker is unhappy because he expected a Christmas bonus, but didn't get it. This man is envious of another and is therefore unhappy. He would like very much to possess a quality he sees in his neighbor. His expectations have not materialized, and he is unhappy. A gambler is unhappy because he lost money when obviously expected to win a fortune. A man goes into deep depression when he is told he has terminal cancer. For as long as he expects to live a healthy life, he will remain unhappy and perhaps die a miserable death.

I could find countless examples of unhappy moments and incidents that all have some sort of unfulfilled expectation as the prime cause of unhappiness. Their number would fill hundreds of volumes. I once asked a group of thirty young people to look into their lives and try to find even one unhappy moment that could not ultimately be traced to an unfulfilled expectation. They were unable to come up with even a single incident. I have asked numerous old people to do the same and they have been no more successful than the teenagers. As far as I can see, all unfulfilled expectations lead to some form of unhappiness.

If this is so, the effects and consequences are great and far-reaching indeed. If it is true that unfulfilled expectations cause unhappiness, is it then possible to eliminate much of the unhappiness in our lives by looking more closely into and perhaps revising some of our own expectations? I think so. Surely, an indispensable ingredient to happiness is contentment, and contentment is not possible, so long as there are many and great unfulfilled expectations. If a man is restless and not satisfied with what he has and with what he is, then, you can be sure that he is in for lots of unhappiness.

But here is where we run into a serious problem. All of us need to have expectations. We dream dreams and have visions of a better tomorrow. Expectations are a motivating force in our lives. They make us move. They drive us to things. They make life's trials and tribulations meaningful and worthwhile. A man without expectations is worse than a vegetable. He is barely alive. Surely then, many of our expectations will remain unfulfilled and many of our desires unrealized. This is true and perhaps this is why there is more than meets the eye in the old saying: "happiness is not of this world."

I believe, however, that we can avoid much unhappiness if we can eliminate unrealistic and unreasonable expectations from our lives. To expect a painless and trouble-free life is an unrealistic expectation that cannot materialize. The teenager who expects to always find his sweetheart smiling and in high spirits is bound to be disappointed. He who expects a high standard of living on a meager salary is also asking for unhappiness and disappointment. If, on the other hand, I expect my life to be a mixture of success and failure, I will not be as hurt and as disappointed when I experience frustrations. I expected them, and now they are here. Those "let-down" feelings are kept to a minimum. If I expect that I will be misunderstood by people time and time again, when it does happen, I am not deeply hurt. Although most of us know that we cannot always be understood by everybody, the fact remains that we expect to be understood always and by everybody. And that is what makes us unhappy.

It is important then, if we are to be happy, to examine and, if necessary, re-evaluate our expectations of people, of life and of ourselves. If our expectations are unrealistic, then, we can be sure that we are walking into unhappy days ahead. If our expectations are outrageous, we are surely candidates for depression. If we make impossible demands upon ourselves, we can expect to be unhappy.

If, on the other hand, we somehow keep ourselves, our friends and our lives in proper perspective, we can draw up a list of expectations that stand a good chance of being fulfilled. Consequently, we can be reasonably assured of a relatively happy life.

This book is an attempt to help people gain a few new insights into love and marriage. If only it can aid each reader to be more realistic of one's expectations of love and marriage, I will have succeeded and will be happy and content.

BOB GARON (1979)

THE MAGIC OF LOVE

Intimacy is a precious gift. It is something strangers dream about, sweethearts hope for, and lovers enjoy. Yet, despite the fact that it is desired by so many, intimacy does not mean the same to everybody.

Some associate intimacy, first and foremost, with the physical act of lovemaking. I have often heard women say: "Bob, we're so close to each other that we have even been to bed together." We use the expression "to be intimate with …" to imply that there has been some sort of sexual relationship. Many people fail to understand that physical proximity—even sexual union—does not necessarily breed intimacy. In fact, it very often does create disgust and hatred.

For others (and I am one of them) intimacy is a feeling of mutual affinity—of close communion between lovers or friends which comes with time, understanding and love. I am not speaking about the "forced togetherness" that is a marriage of two people, who, for convenience or some social or economic reasons, have given up loving and are merely "living under the same roof." We often mistakenly judge people to be intimate and madly in love just because they have stayed together for so very long.

I believe that people who are intimate form a very strange union of one mind, one heart, but two bodies. In other words, intimacy is a necessary by-product of true love. Any couple living a deep love relationship will naturally and effortlessly benefit from the fruits of intimacy.

Intimacy is not jealous. In fact, it seeks to widen the horizons of the friends or lovers. Its objective is to help each other overcome fears, personality shortcomings and character deficiencies. Intimacy means trusting. Trusting enough to allow others to come close. Trusting enough to share with others while not fearing to lose the loyalty of the beloved.

Intimacy does not mean exclusiveness. It does not mean cutting oneself off from meaningful relations with others. It *does* mean enriching oneself through new friendships.

A man who tries to hoard his loved one; who attempts to keep her all to himself in such a way that she finds herself unable to relate with others in a meaningful way, will find himself sorely disappointed. In a short time, he will have an emotionally dead woman on his hands, for in the stifling atmosphere of jealousy, a person withers and dies.

If you want to attain a high degree of intimacy, you must be willing to invest a lot of time, energy, and especially courage. But even before this, what is needed most is a firm commitment to a person. You must first of all believe in an individual before you can convince yourself to put much into a relationship. If you feel that so-and-so is a poor risk, then you will necessarily conclude that he is not worth all the trouble that true love and the succeeding intimacy demand.

To achieve a high degree of intimacy is one thing. To keep that level is something else again. Intimate friends have been known to become arch enemies. What is needed to safeguard deep intimacy is to build HABITS OF LOVE that will ensure a continued increase of love and trust.

If you are lucky enough to enjoy the intimacy of a friend or lover, do not become complacent. Be careful not to take your relationship for granted. Be at peace in your heart, but do not fall asleep in a false sense of security.

If you are one of those lucky few who has found a true friend and you now share in a vibrant and living intimacy, get the most from it. But, remember, if you are going to get what you are looking for, you will have to put into it ten times more than you expect to receive. It's not easy, but that's the way it is.

WHO ARE YOU?

THE YOUNG WIFE SAT before me weeping bitterly with her face in her hands. Her husband had gone abroad five months before, leaving her behind together with her three children. Now, she had just received news from her friend that her man was having an affair with another woman in that far off land.

"It's not true, Bob," she whispered between heavy sobs, "it just can't be true … I know my husband … he wouldn't do such a thing."

But it *was* true. The husband *was* playing around. In fact, this was only the beginning of a long chain of events that led to the subsequent break-up of their marriage.

On countless occasions, I have met people who have made the tragic mistake of believing that they "really and truly" know a friend, a sweetheart, a relative, a stranger, or a loved one. Their mistakes lie in believing that they have come to know each other.

Very often, we think we know somebody when, in fact, we only know something *about* his family, friends and enemies. We know where he got his education, how long he has been working at his present job and what he intends to do next weekend.

This is not knowing somebody. It's knowing *about* somebody. Knowledge means more than gathering a few or even a multitude of facts. It means putting a lot of things together. It means "figuring out somebody." It means finding out "what makes him tick." It means probing into the heart and soul of a person … with his permission … and *understanding* his behavioral patterns.

In short, knowing a person *really* and *truly* means hard work … lots of it. And what makes it very difficult is the fact that precious few people are willing to allow you close enough to make a decent study of them.

"Why is it," remarked my brother Don, "that when you ask people: 'Who are you?' They always answer by giving you their name, which is really quite empty of much information about them?"

My brother had a very valid point. *He* is a keen observer of people and, having travelled all over the world, he noted how people do their utmost to hide in spite of all the talk of bridging the communication gap and being open with one another.

So you can imagine what a difficult job it is to know a person sufficiently well. It isn't all that easy. I have the opportunity to speak confidentially to countless people who come to me and honestly attempt to tell me about themselves. And even this is not as simple as it sounds.

We have so many built-in defense mechanisms that it very often happens that, in spite of our sincere willingness to open up, we find it impossible because of "something inside" which holds us back and prevents us from doing so.

Then there is the lack of *real* confidence in ourselves and in others that prevents us from opening our hearts to the gaze of outsiders. There is that fear of getting hurt, of being rejected, and of revealing our weaknesses to potential enemies that almost forces us to "keep it all inside."

Perhaps what makes a person so hard to know is the fact, the undeniable fact, that people are constantly changing, and changing rapidly.

You may know me today, but, unless you stay close to me, you may not know me tomorrow. In fact, unless I am completely blank, I will somehow most certainly change tomorrow.

What our poor little wife at the beginning of the column failed to realize is that five months abroad certainly had to change her husband in some way. Perhaps he had no thought of fooling around before leaving. Perhaps he had never seen what he saw and felt what he felt in that far off land before. Perhaps the man went through so many changes that unfaithfulness was no longer so difficult nor so forbidding.

I suppose it isn't all that mysterious. You cannot expect a young man who has been married and who has three children not to have changed over the years. I guess you should not be too surprised, then, if a teenager goes off to war and after having seen so much violence and having dipped his hand in blood, comes back a changed man.

I personally believe that we change every day. True, we all possess a basic psychological and emotional structure which remains pretty much static throughout our lives. However, there are countless factors that bring about innumerable changes within us.

The simple fact of growing older necessitates changes. When a child grows into adolescence, he must change … if only to be accepted by his peers. And when he moves into adulthood, he is expected to change again. If he does not, he is constantly reminded that he is just a "big kid" and he had better "grow up and get with it."

These changes are not simple nor few. They are many and complex. And they cut deeply into a man's heart.

This is what makes friendship and love so exciting and such a great adventure. I have often said that what makes love so worthwhile is the "joy of discovery." It is the fun of finding another in the real sense of the word that gives an exotic taste to courtship.

I have also often said (and it bears repeating here) that when two people get bored with one another, it is because they have stopped "discovering each other." And when that happens it means big trouble ahead.

We take too much for granted. We think too much of our ability to know others. We jump to conclusions and before long, we have neatly classified people and placed them in easy-to-find categories.

The result is very often tragic. Whenever we deal with people, we run the terrible risk of miscalculation.

In international relations, miscalculation can lead to war. When one nation believes that the other will back away in a showdown, and it does not, then there is shooting.

In human relations, when a person is guilty of a miscalculation, it often means the end of a friendship or in the very least, that somebody gets hurt. Though we do not like to admit it, we do miscalculate time and time again. He whom we believe to be a friend, turns against us viciously. He whom we thought to be loyal and true walks away in times of stress and hardship. He whom we were so sure of, turns out to be unsteady. And he whom we least expected, stands by us through thick and thin.

This has been my experience again and again. It is for this reason that I am very cautious now with people I take into my confidence. On the other hand, I am more willing and disposed to take risks with people who may not impress me very well in the beginning. In other words, I am more open than ever and I believe I should be quick to forgive and to overlook many little things in order to better understand a person.

Miscalculation usually means a false judgement that ends up hurting people and closing minds tightly. The tragedy lies in the fact that when we make ourselves out to be experts on people, we tend to fall into the very real temptation of making snap judgements concerning them.

Sometimes our discussions are off the mark because of lack of information or misinformation.

Perhaps it is good to remember that when we approach people, we are dealing with unbelievably complex and sensitive creatures that should not be taken lightly or for granted.

LOVE IS NOT BLIND

There are exceptional instances in which a person, due to mental illness, undergoes a radical personality change after marriage that could not be foreseen. Aside from such exceptional cases, a person's basic personality is firmly fixed by the time he or she comes to marriageable age. In a courtship of any reasonable length of time, one's basic personality can be recognized by the other party - if he or she has open eyes.

Unfortunately, love-or physical infatuation- is a great eye closer and a great rationalizer. "I know he drinks a little." (he is tipsy on half of their dates), "but that's just because he is so shy; he'll be alright once we're married." "Sure, she's kind of bossy, but she's such a sweet kid, you don't mind that; and once we're married, I'll wear pants." "He does fly into a temper over such little things and it seems that we're always quarreling; but he's nervous and high strung. Marriage will change that." "Gosh, she's jealous! I can hardly kiss my own sister. But I suppose she's afraid she might lose me; after we're married she'll be different."

We all have heard such wishful thinking. Sometimes it is because physical desire has put reason to sleep. Sometimes it is because the person is so anxious to get married that he or she will settle for almost any kind of partner who comes along.

Then too, there are the pathological cases: the mother-dominated son who unconsciously seeks a wife who will dominate him; the girl who is driven by unrecognized guilt feelings to choose a brutal husband who will provide the punishment she unconsciously craves.

Original sin has disturbed the control that reason should exert over the biological urge, so it is perhaps not too surprising that many young men and women walk blindly into a marriage doomed to unhappiness; they walk into it in spite of the danger signals that are obvious for any intelligent person to see. The alcoholic husband, the nagging wives, the vicious-tempered men and the insanely jealous women: they suddenly didn't develop their undesirable traits after marriage. And the naïve belief that "I can get him (or her) to change," flies in the face of all the psychological evidence, the evidence that a person's basic personality pattern does not change after maturity. A person may grow in virtue with the years, but deep-seated emotional and psychological disorders usually will grow worse, barring a miracle of course, and few miracles of this kind occur.

Fortunately, those who see marriage as a vocation (and thank God their number is legion) do retain some vestiges of discrimination and do try to make a wise and prayerful choice. They not only ask, "Will he (she) and I have fun together?" They also ask, "Will he be a good father (or she a good mother) for my children?"

However, even in the great multitude of normally happy marriages there are sometimes areas of stress which occur from the mistaken idea that another person can change his personality at his or her command. An important ingredient of happiness in marriage is the willingness to accept each other "as we are." The perfect match is a rare phenomenon. Almost inevitably, there will be personality differences, clashes of temperament. The need is to adjust to these differences rather than to expect to change them.

If a wife is by nature a poor manager, no amount of griping is going to make her a smart budgeter and an efficient housekeeper. It will be a happier marriage if the husband will accept and love her as she is, and quietly do his best to make up for her deficiencies (as she almost certainly is making up for his). If a husband is by nature a quiet stay-at-home type of person, no amount of complaining is going to change him into a party-going crowd-loving individual. A vivacious wife may find this is a trial, but it will be a happier marriage if she cheerfully accepts the fact and stops trying to make the man over. The wife may be an inordinately neat individual who can't stand the sight of a pin out of place, and her husband, a sloppy fellow who never puts things away. The man may be an obsessively punctual person who wants everything on the dot and the wife a flighty person who never has dinner ready on time.

"You have your faults and I have mine. Let's just accept each other as we are. Let's be willing to settle for the good that we find in each other (and look for the good) so that under God, ours may be a happier home." That is a simple and yet infallible philosophy upon which to build a day-by-day, satisfying marriage. Blessed will the children be who grow up in the peace and the charity of such a home.

A LASTING FRIENDSHIP

AN IMPORTANT QUESTION about friendship just popped into my mind. If you have ever given any thought to what makes a friendship click, then perhaps you have asked yourself the same question.

Why is it that very few friendships are long-lasting? If you look around, you will find precious few deep and lasting friendships. You will notice that in your lives (and in the lives of those you are a little familiar with) relatively few people ever keep a true friend for any great length of time.

Most succeed in getting "close" for a while, only to break up or drift away after a time. It seems that just when you believe that "you've got a friend," something happens and gets things all fouled up. Just when you think that you can really trust this person, there is a terrible misunderstanding that spoils everything and draws you apart from one another.

Why is it that most people are just miserable failures when it comes to building a lasting friendship?

I think that it is because of the very delicate nature of a friendship. Friendship is just another word for love.

The question asked also holds true for love. True friendship is "liking pushed beyond its limits and across the boundary of love."

Deep friendship is synonymous with deep love. Friendship, like love, varies in degree and intensity. Falling out of friendship is the same as falling out of love.

When a love relationship begins to break up, the first thing you can notice is the communication breakdown that has taken place. You can see how a couple no longer spends much time in meaningful dialogue. This is either out of necessity or actual intent. This lack of communication gives rise to an ever-increasing number of conflicts and tensions due to those inevitable misunderstandings that can never be corrected properly because there is insufficient dialogue. This sad situation causes the relationship to deteriorate further until things become so messy that major surgery is needed. If this does not take place quickly, then the inevitable "split" occurs and we have another friendship down the drain.

The reason, I think, that so many friendships do not go the route is that most people don't take time. We expect too much for nothing. We hope for a huge return on a tiny investment. We think that all we have to do is plant a seed, walk away, wait a while, and then come back and harvest a friendship.

Sorry! That's not the way things work out. It takes time and a lot of blood, sweat and tears to succeed in keeping the lifelong friendship intact. It calls for a protracted effort.

When I get back to the States, I will have to begin rebuilding old friendships and rekindling the fires of loves that have died because of time, distance and neglect.

Deep friendships are not for busy men. Perhaps that is the reason why great men are so alone. They don't have the time needed for deep friendships.

A friend once wrote to me: "friendship is a plant of slow growth. May those vines binding us together have strong roots in the soil of our hearts." He is so right.

If you want to have a deep, long-lasting friendship, take the time.

LETTER TO A JEALOUS WIFE

Dear Trixie:

I read with interest and, at the same time, sadness, the letter you wrote telling me about your hurt feelings and your subsequent behavior.

You and Leon have been married for only three years. I can see that, in spite of this short span of time, your union is heading for big trouble unless there are some changes made-and made soon.

I know you get hurt when Leon talks to a pretty girl or gives another woman some attention. I've had a long talk with your husband, and now, after hearing both sides, I think I am in a position to write something substantial.

First, let me tell you Trixie, that I strongly believe that jealousy is essentially an attitude of mistrust. I say "attitude" because a person isn't jealous one day and not jealous the next. A jealous woman is always jealous. It's just that there are times when the signs of this "state of mind" become apparent and obvious because they gush to the surface and explode into the open.

I said, jealousy is "an attitude of mistrust" because it is clear to me that a jealous woman does not really trust her husband. She may say she does, but her behavior directly contradicts her words. The fact is that the jealous wife is deathly *afraid.* Afraid of coming out second best in her daily competition with other women for the heart and mind of her husband. Afraid to grow old and wrinkled. Afraid to see her husband in the presence of women more beautiful than she. Afraid to have her husband meet females of greater intellectual capacity. Afraid of losing her charm. In short, afraid of losing her man.

Because of this fear, the jealous woman makes desperate attempts to cut off from the circle of her husband's friends those women whom she feels are threats to her security. I say "desperately" because some of her actions are obviously clumsy and quite clear to even the unobserving eye. And I believe, Trixie, that you are becoming such a woman.

Leon has told me that you have flown into a rage at the sight of him talking to an office-mate. You have accused him (and I purposely use the word "accused") of having affairs with women he hardly knows, much less loves. You have publicly shown your displeasure with some of his most innocent social contacts with women. You have, finally, in the words of your husband, begun "to make life miserable" for him.

Leon has reacted in typical male fashion. You told me that he is irritable and cranky and unapproachable lately. You said you thought it was because there's someone else; that he is in love with "an unknown woman." I assure you, Trixie, that this is not so. Leon loves you and only YOU. However, your constant mistrust of him, your apparent lack of confidence in him, your attempts to, as he puts it, "guard him"; all these things have made him a frustrated man.

I say frustrated because Leon has been trying very hard to prove to you that you are the only woman in his life. But, try as he may, he just can't seem to convince you. And in spite of the fact that you can't prove nor even begin to prove any kind of infidelity whatsoever, you still persist in your groundless suspicions of him.

Trixie don't get hurt, but I feel I must tell you the truth. You are, without a doubt, a very jealous woman. This is not an accusation. It's just a simple fact. I say it because I'm your friend and because I would like to see your marriage strengthened and happy.

However, unless there is a change of attitude, I fear that there will be heavy seas ahead. And the stormy weather may drive your marriage onto the rocks. Every man (like every woman) has a breaking point, a "frustration breaking point." Leon is fast approaching the mark and unless something is done to head him off, I fear that both of you are on an inevitable collision course which is sure to bring about an end to your marriage.

I hope you will listen to me, Trixie, and believe me. You must show more trust in your husband. You must allow him more freedom. You must call off the guards. You must give him the liberty to prove himself to you.

Deep in your heart, I know this will be difficult. However, I hope for both your sakes it will not be impossible. Though you may not feel confidence, you must show it. Your husband must feel that you trust him, even if you don't. Believe me Trixie, you will notice a great change come over your husband should you be able to do what I'm suggesting. He will feel that perhaps there will be an end to his frustrations; that perhaps you are beginning to believe what he knows to be the truth; that perhaps the baseless suspicions will finally cease. In other words, Leon may just begin to feel the oneness of mind and heart that lovers are meant to have and without which their love cannot survive.

Finally, Trixie, please believe me when I say, in all sincerity, that I'm not taking sides. Please don't doubt me if I tell you that I understand your husband as a man understands a man. Sometimes the best way to keep the thieves away is by pretending that there's nothing of value in your house. When you begin to build walls and station armed guards around your home, then very potential robber begins to wonder what is it that you have that calls for such elaborate security measures.

This is one time when trying too hard to hold a man will insure complete failure.

I care.

BOB

PARALYSIS SETS INTO MARRIAGE

JERRY HAS BEEN MARRIED for the past seven years to a beautiful woman named Cora. They have two children. Right now, Jerry is happy that he does not have more. Why? Because he is thinking of leaving his wife.

The last five years have been very unhappy for Jerry and Cora. Constant bickering and quarreling have slowly eroded their once-beautiful love. Hardly a day passes without some sort of conflict, and tension is almost always there.

Oh yes, both have tried hard enough. In fact, this seems to be part of the problem. After so many attempts, so many good resolutions, so many reconciliations, there seems to be hardly any progress. Try as they may, things hardly ever work out for them. They just cannot seem to solve any of the major problems in their marriage. The constant bickering and quarreling have sapped their strength and made their love very anemic indeed.

Jerry used to think that given a little time everything would be alright. He believed that it was just a question of adaptation and a little bit of goodwill. He was sure that sooner or later both of them would find that marital peace and harmony they desperately longed for.

Now Jerry has almost reached the conclusion that there is no solution and that all is hopeless. For the first time since his wedding day, he is beginning to think of finding himself another woman. It's not that Jerry is an evil, immoral and dissolute young man. I suppose you could say that he is just sick and tired of trying. He is fed up with going through the same old exercise in frustration time and time again. He feels that no matter what happens, things will always be the same with him and Cora. In other words, he feels the paralysis of frustration creeping into their marriage.

Of all the martial problems possible, perhaps the most dangerous is that unresolved frustration that becomes a daily routine in the lives of a couple. It is most tragic because it kills all hope. And when hope for something better disappears, the despair and vision of an even unhappier life usually set in; and when this happens, people feel trapped. Then, like flies caught in the spider's web, they struggle madly to free themselves.

For this reason, it is of prime importance that married couples (friends and sweethearts, too!) work hard at making some headway in the solutions to their problems-even if it is only token progress.

When a husband and a wife keep knocking their heads together in fruitless attempts to effect a change, they begin to hurt badly and start to lose courage. Whenever there is trouble, both parties have to make sure that there is some kind of movement towards a positive solution. This is an absolute MUST.

Men look for this more than do women. Perhaps it is because males have a lower threshold of suffering than females. Maybe it is also because men tend to analyze situations and look for answers. Women, on the other hand, are endowed with much greater patience. Their thinking is very often clouded by strong emotions. Consequently, they can bear frustration with more dignity and for a much longer time than men.

However, this last quality also has its disadvantages. Women often believe that men can take it as much as they themselves can. Here, they are sorely mistaken. The male is usually the first to throw up his hands in complete frustration and walk away.

People who really care about saving their relationship should, if needs be, give in somewhere along the line when they realize that the paralysis of frustration is setting in. One of the parties should be concerned enough and have the humility to step back, if only to encourage the other to keep on trying.

What I, as a counsellor, fear most when advising couples in trouble is that one of them gets fed up and suddenly stops trying. Then, even if there is a solution in sight, their love is doomed.

Always remember that what makes love living and vibrant is the expectation of ever-increasing happiness. The moment this hope is shattered, you can prepare yourself for the tragic end of a marriage.

THE WORKING MALE

I REMEMBER LISTENING to Dean Ulgado during a symposium at San Beda College some years ago. Speaking about the role of the Filipino husband, he stated that his number one priority is "to earn."

The most degrading accusation that you can level at a Filipino father is that he is a terrible "breadwinner." The Filipino male who can bring home a fat pay check and who can earn enough to send his kids to a "good school" is looked upon with great admiration and, at times, even awe.

However, the Filipino male is not unique in this respect. In fact, in just about every corner of the globe, man's success is often measured by his ability to provide for his family. From the dark jungles of Africa where the skillful hunter is respected for his consistently fruitful hunts, to the great urban centers of North America where to be a highly paid executive is the ultimate success, the male is thought of as a strong family man if he can "bring home the bacon."

This makes things hard on a man. Whereas a woman has the family to keep her occupied full time, the male must both spend a full day earning a living in a highly competitive world and all the while play a vital role in the family life at home. The truth of the matter is that most responsible men are torn between their dual roles of breadwinners and fathers.

Very often, an anxious wife faces a terrible dilemma. Her husband has to work time and half to earn enough. But she would also like to see him more involved in the home life of the family. Most men cannot do both well. Usually, one aspect suffers.

Ordinarily, when a man has to choose between his work and his family, the family can be expected to come out on the losing end. This may be very difficult for the wife to accept. She may begin to feel that her husband no longer cares about her and the children. She may even suspect that her husband lives his life only for his job and that his home comes in a distant second in the order of his priorities.

In a way, if a man is so determined in his pursuit of success, the woman is, in great part, to blame. A wife expects a man to succeed. She surely hopes to have the money needed every month to keep the family functioning well. This means that the husband must get out into a very competitive world and earn. And sometimes this can take ninety percent of his time. Often, increasing success means decreasing time for the family.

When a wife feels she is losing her husband to his job and begins to actively challenge his commitment and compete with his work, she creates a very real problem.

The man is torn between his home and his office and suddenly finds that he is less effective in both areas.

The answer to this problem is not easy. A detailed study of a man's job and its relationship with his family is in order. The family must prosper financially, emotionally, and psychologically. It is for the couple to come to concrete conclusions about their dilemma and make the corresponding adjustments. Sometimes the action to be taken may have to be drastic. Perhaps the husband will have to limit his success in the office in order not to be a failure in the home. On the other hand, he may have to admit that the question of economic survival has forced him to almost completely surrender his duties at home.

WOMAN'S POWERFUL WEAKNESSES

A MAN DOES NOT have to be big to be strong; and a woman need not be tiny to be weak. Very often, a weakness can be turned into a winning factor in this complex game of life.

Woman, who is supposed to be of the weaker sex, uses many techniques to gain superiority over the stronger sex. Woman is usually bargaining from an inferior position in terms of brute strength. And she knows it too. She understands this so well that she has learned to make the most of her drawback and use it to get plenty of leverage in any conflict she is engaged in with man.

Take what I call "NAWASA power." That is, weeping and crying. Woman knows that tears contain chemicals that can, among other things, melt a man's heart and transform the bitterness in his attitude into a sweet disposition. She has learned this from her youth and has used her knowledge to advantage. How many men have said: "Alright, well do it your way" or "Stop crying, if that's what you want, it's okay by me."

When a man sees a woman cry, he tends to think that some catastrophe of major proportions has come upon him. Because tears do not come easily to him, he often forgets that tears can be turned on or off at will by most females. Ever since the beginning of time, woman has used her "NAWASA power" to her great advantage.

Another technique woman uses in order to get what she wants is nagging. By constantly repeating the same request over and over again she can drive a man to giving in to her desires by forcing him into submission. A man who is the unfortunate victim of an expert nagger will do just about anything to get even one moment of peace. How many big men have gone down silently to infamous defeat at the hands of a "little nagger?"

Another method that woman uses to get what she wants is ridicule. By laughing at him (and there are countless subtle ways of laughing at a man) woman hits him at his weakest point—his vanity. She can just about destroy a man by continuously knocking him down.

Every time she brings him to his knees by laughing at him, she is wounding his vanity. Man is extremely sensitive on this point and more than one has been completely crushed in this way by a "little woman."

Another method woman uses to get her way is that of indecision. She refuses to come to a decision that is clearly hers to make. The man, in complete exasperation, then keeps fishing around for something that will please her. In the end, he will suggest what she wanted in the first place and she will then agree to it. But she is making it come from him.

Perhaps one of woman's most powerful weapons is her refusal to give herself sexually to her mate. She knows she is sexually attractive. She is fully aware of man's intense sexual drive and she uses her physical attributes expertly not only to entice man but also to keep him in line by threatening to withhold her sexual participation. Countless husbands have come to know this through painful frustration and by being sexually deprived of their mate's body.

Because these are strong measures, they often backfire and explode in woman's face. She has gone too far and her efforts have proved to be self-defeating more than once.

Regardless, woman has shown herself to be a powerful and formidable "weakling."

HOLD YOUR FIRE

BILLY AND RUDY HAD BEEN close friends for three years. They had spent long hours together in intense conversations, exchanging thoughts and experiencing deeply personal feelings. They revealed themselves to one another in many deeply moving personal encounters.

Billy and Rudy were not teenagers. They were grown men in their late twenties who considered themselves mature and emotionally solid. In fact, they felt that their friendship for one another was so deeply rooted that nothing and nobody could shake its foundations. Nothing and nobody did—until one fateful morning when Billy was talking to a friend in the office.

His business associate just happened to mention in a casual conversation that Rudy had said some pretty nasty things about him during a party one evening. Billy was deeply hurt. How could Rudy utter such terrible words? After all these years? And behind his back, too!

Billy was boiling mad. He sat down and dashed off a very insulting letter to Rudy. In it, he wrote many things he meant and many more that he did not really believe, but were only designed to hurt.

When Rudy got the letter, he felt great confusion, then deep disappointment. What he had had said about his friend had not been reported truthfully. Yes, he had spoken about Billy, but not in the way it was recounted to his friend. In fact, Rudy was surprised that his confidant, who had shared so much with him for so long, would even entertain such talk.

As things worked out in the end, Billy and Rudy were reconciled. But only after a lot of hurt feelings and plenty of explanations and apologies.

What is sad about the incident above is that it really wasn't necessary and could have been avoided. Most of us are quick on the trigger. We shoot and ask questions later. Sometimes it's too late. You can hardly apologize to a corpse.

The problem with most of us is that we really do not trust very much nor very easily. Often, we feel we are being attacked when, in reality, there is no real threat. Sometimes, our enemies are mere fabrications of our minds. We feel so insecure that we are quickly and easily put on the defensive. I guess we are a little like children afraid of the darkness and who are wandering in the forest at night.

If we could only trust people—especially our friend—enough to withhold judgment until we get a clear view of things; if we could only hold our fire until we are sure our target is really a foe; if we could only do this, we could and would avoid a lot of emotional and psychological carnage.

Giving a man a chance to defend himself, to explain his side before condemning him and sentencing him is a principle of democracy that we hold dear. Regrettably, we are often guilty of violating this precious safeguard in our relations with our associates and friends. I am the first to admit to this-and to the needless pain it has caused me and those I love.

"Innocent until proven guilty" is a principle of law. We would do well to apply it to our lives and to those we cherish-and even to those we do not especially care for.

How often does a useless skirmish break out between husband and wife, parent and child, office mates and just plain friends because someone is "trigger happy"?

It is easy to say you are sorry after the harm has been done. It is harder to stop the bleeding. It is almost impossible to eliminate the scars occasioned by such words. Plastic surgery is both costly and time-consuming. It is best to avoid the clash in the first place.

However, we are all very impulsive and we often react too quickly. Inevitably, this over-reaction causes many innocent people to get hurt. And, tragically enough, some of the damage is irreparable.

I have hurt far too many by being too quick to strike. Many unsuspecting loved ones have been caught in the line of fire. I am sharing these thoughts with you in the hope that you may learn from my impulsiveness. Keep calm. Think. And please … hold your fire.

THE GOOD OLD DAYS

Manny and Menchie were at it again … Same old argument. Same old conclusion. Same old wound opened again.

Feeling completely frustrated and helpless, Manny retired to his room, where he sat down on the side of the bed and put his face in his hands.

Menchie came in softly, sat down beside him, leaned her head on his shoulder and said:

"What has happened to us, Manny? Three years of marriage and we seem to be growing apart from one another."

"Yeah," said Manny, in a whisper, "it isn't like the good old days anymore, is it?"

So many couples like Manny and Menchie look back upon their days of courtship with great longing and, at the same time, with a certain amount of pain. Pain, because it hurts to see how far they have regressed in their love for one another. Because, as the song goes, "those were the days my friend, we thought would never end." But they did.

There is a longing for those days, because it was then that both appeared to understand each other. Why did things go so smoothly then? Because they really opened up to one another; because they spent long hours probing each other's mind and heart; because there were no secrets between them; because they were frank and truthful with each other.

Things were wonderful then because there was the thrill and excitement of discovery. To look into the deepest recesses of a loved one's heart is just about the most memorable adventure in a man or woman's life. With every date came new discoveries, new realizations. Every intense conversation revealed hidden beauties never before suspected.

It was this expectation, this "what-will-I-find next" attitude that made courtship so exciting. It was piecing together the personality and the heart of the loved one that was such an enjoyable challenge. Most of all, it was the exhilarating feeling of security one felt in knowing that here, among the millions of people the world over "is a man I understand and who reads me like an open book. (And who loves me dearly despite my stupidities.)"

If countless people down through the years have been inspired by the touching romance of a Romeo and a Juliet, it is because there is in all of us that overwhelming desire to reach out to another person and to know him truly and authentically. And there is in all of us the corresponding longing to be reached in the same sincere way. However, this is such a rare happening that when we see it portrayed on the silver screen, we all identify with Romy and Julie.

If so many couples are unhappy and disillusioned after a few years of marriage, it is because they have forgotten how to court, it is because they do not realize that when two people get married, courtship does not end. On the contrary, it is supposed to shift into high gear.

If so many husbands and wives are bored with one another, it is because, like a basketball team that is over-confident, they have relaxed their play. And, because of this let-up in effort; they soon find themselves disoriented, confused, demoralized and far behind.

If there are so many unhappy marriages, it is because couples have forgotten the very slight difference between courtship and marriage. Courtship is a "couple-of days-a-week affair. Marriage is a 24-hour-a-day courtship.

THE FOLLY OF SECRET MARRIAGES

THE WHOLE FAMILY SAT in stunned silence, unable and unwilling to believe their ears. It just could not be true. Yet, there was no denying the marriage contract on the kitchen table. Marilou, their 19-year-old daughter, was indeed married to Manolo, that 20-year-old high school drop-out they disliked so intensely.

In fact, the two young people had been married secretly three months before by a judge in the neighboring municipality. During the twelve weeks that had elapsed since then, Marilou and Manolo had told nobody except three intimate friends. Their behavior never gave rise to the slightest suspicion. As a result, their announcement had caught everybody by complete surprise.

Secret marriages are very common here in the Philippines. In my daily counselling, I regularly meet young people who have contracted marriage without the knowledge and consent of their parents. In fact, I find that few young people have qualms of conscience about forging the consent papers if they are under age.

I don't like secret marriages. In fact, I always try to discourage them. I have repeatedly refused to marry people secretly, and unless an engaged couple can give me at least one very solid reason, I will continue to dissuade young people from doing so. I must readily admit, though, that there are some valid circumstances that could call for secrecy. However, they are the rare exceptions rather than the general rule.

Why do teenagers and young adults go off and marry secretly? For many reasons, I suppose. But, in my experience, I have found that parental objections and the desire "to secure one another" are, by far, the most often cited.

If I were a parent—and I'm not—I would tone down harsh and bitter criticism of my teenager's sweetheart. Police methods work sometimes, but, any thinking adult can tell you, they most often backfire.

I honestly believe that some parents are so brutal and unkind in their opposition to their daughter's courtship that they very often push the frustrated girl into a wedding she doesn't *really* want. I have seen teenagers provoked into a marriage that is merely an act of rebellion-all to their subsequent regret.

When people get frightened, they often do things they would not think of doing under normal circumstances. And when two teenagers, who believe (rightly or wrongly) they madly love one another, feel their love is threatened, then anything can happen-and usually does.

Most often, if they are convinced that their parents have a reasonable chance of separating them, they will simply run off and sleep together one night and thereby force mom and dad to allow their marriage. Or they go to a judge, falsify their ages, or forge their parents' consent and get secretly married.

Another common reason given for secret marriages is that of the need for mutual security.

"Bob, we got married to be sure of each other."

How often have I heard this statement coming from young people? However, getting secretly married "to be sure of each other" is really quite ridiculous and illogical.

You don't marry a man you're not sure of. In fact, you prolong the courtship until you can be reasonably sure. Saying "I do' before a priest or a judge does not, as many separated people can testify, assure a happy marriage.

I don't like secret marriages for a number of reasons. First of all, they are usually rush jobs done under tremendous pressure and unbearable tension. And when people act in such conditions, they usually make mistakes.

Then, think of the awkward situation secretly married couples find themselves in. They are very much married but by force of circumstances they must be married but by force of circumstances they must continue to lead the life of single people. They live in constant fear of being discovered. Their lives are just one big bundle of tension. The first years of marriage are tough enough without adding these complications.

So many young people think a secret marriage is a quick and easy solution to a problem. More often than not, it merely marks the beginning of a long life of pain and regret.

THE LIFE OF AN ESTRANGED SPOUSE ISN'T EASY

SUSAN IS 26 YEARS-OLD and very pretty. She graduated from an exclusive school for girls at the top of her class. Because of her sparkling personality, she had no difficulty finding a good job with an advertising firm.

Needless to say, there are many young men (and older men) who find her extremely attractive and attempt to date her. In short, Susan seems to have everything a girl looks for in life. She also has two handsome children. Susan is married. However, 3 years ago, she joined the ever-growing ranks of separated women.

Susan is typical of many unhappy young females whose lives have been completely turned around because of a marriage that did not work out. She is only one of those countless miserable human beings who are caught up in such a very desperate situation of life that it just about defies solution.

Susan's courtship began pretty much like all the others. She was a beautiful and attractive coed actively participating in most school projects. Mario was a handsome guy who knew how to court girls very effectively. In fact, most women dreamed of falling in love with him. You could not blame Susan for thinking herself the luckiest girl in town when Mario asked her to go steady.

He was such a gentleman. Always so kind and so considerate. And, of course, so polite. It was a whirlwind courtship that lasted seven months. Parties, movies, picnics, and home visits. The parents did not object and the marriage date was set.

After the wedding, the happy couple moved into a room in the parents' house. The first ten months were very happy for Susan. She delivered a baby boy and Mario was about ready to graduate from school. There were occasional quarrels but nothing very serious.

Then it happened. Mario began to stay out late at right. Sometimes he could come home at one or two in the morning. Susan asked him why the late hours. He gave her all kinds of weak excuses.

He became cold and indifferent to her. And he picked arguments with her at the slightest provocation. They began shouting at each other. His parents began nagging their daughter-in-law and accusing her of impatience and lack of understanding.

Things went so badly that by the time their second wedding anniversary slipped upon them, and their second child (a girl this time) had been born, they were no longer on speaking terms. Mario began courting girls openly. Susan hated her in-laws, whom she felt always defended her wayward husband.

Finally, the inevitable happened. She left the house with her children and went home to her parents, who advised her never to return.

Oh, yes! Some well-meaning people tried to patch up the broken relationship, but they only made things worse. They were sincere, but totally unequal to the task. Then, two and one half years (and two babies) later, it was all over.

At 23, Susan was separated woman—commanded by the law of the Church and the State, to live alone for the rest of her days. Her only hope of getting a legitimate husband for herself and a father for her children—an early death of Mario.

Almost every day, I counsel at least one separated husband and wife. After seeing this endless procession of miserable people and listening to their countless sufferings, I thought I should write a column about them to plead for more understanding.

I guess the terrible tragedy of a broken marriage must hit close to home for one to fully realize the immense scope of the problem. I have a sister—the eldest in the family and the only girl—who is divorced.

Perhaps it is because of this painful experience that I have a very soft spot in my heart for separated men and women. And, of course, there are those cute children of the broken marriage who are moving rapidly right straight into adolescence and its countless problems.

Let's face it, society is very hard on the separated husband. Harder still on the estranged wife! We expect a young mother who has left her husband to be just that - a dedicated mother (and father too) for the rest of her years.

In her middle age and in the sunset of her years, we demand that she give herself wholly and completely to her grandchildren. We conveniently forget that to be a good mother and a happy grandmother is an exceedingly difficult task without a wonderful father and a contended grandfather.

We so often think solely of the children and forget that the separated woman has a wounded heart which needs TLC (Tender Loving Care) in order to heal decently. We forget that any heart that has received such a heavy blow is going to be scarred for life.

In theory and in conversation, everybody says: "she's only human." But let her try to be human and see what happens. Let her fall in love again and then listen to the talk and gossip begin to build up into a loud roar that is deafening. Let a separated woman be seen with another man and watch what happens to her already damaged reputation—boom!

A while back a 30-year-old separated woman was gunned down in her home by a man with whom she allegedly was "having an affair." The whole incident was given more than enough space in the press.

Newspapers know what people like to read, and they usually give them what they like. So they reported the whole mess in all its gory details. A front page picture showed the half-naked woman lying dead in the pool of her own blood. The accompanying story dwelt on the affair she was supposedly having with the man.

You should have heard people buzz about the whole thing-and enjoy it too!

"How could she?"

"She should not have fooled around."

"She got what she deserved.

"Think about the kids."

I am thinking of how her son will feel when he grows up to be a wonderful teenager and courts a girl. I wonder what she and her concerned parents will think and say when they find out that his mother "was separated"... and "had an affair" ... and "was shot and killed by her lover?"

Do you think the kids will ever be able to walk away from the dirty scandal that haunts them? I don' think so! We "good people" won't let them forget.

A separated woman who is a Catholic and has a Church wedding is torn between two compelling laws. The law of God (and, in this country, the State) which forbids any subsequent marriage or intimate relationship with another man until the death of the spouse.

On the other hand, there is that thoroughly human law within her that says: "You are not an island ... you need to love and to be loved, to have someone ... and your children ..."

And there lies the conflict, and the pain and the sacrifice and the tears. That terrible pulling and pushing that is going on in the inner depths of a wounded heart is what most of us fail to see or understand. For this reason, we are very often hard as nails, condemning and unsympathetic in our judgement.

I know many separated people who have remarried and are extremely restless because they cannot receive the sacraments. They are living good clean lives, but suffer deeply because of this "God vacuum" in their everyday existence.

I watched my sister trying to live alone after 10 years of unhappy married life. Two years later, at the age of 31, and after much soul-searching, she "re-married"

Seven years and one son later, her second husband shot himself. With her little boy, she again stands alone.

Do not get me wrong! I am not advocating divorce. I am not excusing anybody. Nor am I condoning evil and encouraging it. I am a simple guy and it is not for me to change Church and State rules and regulations.

I am only begging for a little understanding and patience for those separated men and women among us. Their lives are tragic and painful enough. We should either extend a helping hand and a sympathetic heart or at least not add to their already enormous burdens. And if we are incapable of any of this, we should stand back in reverent silence and let them suffer in peace.

About the most we can do is accept them just the way they are and help them with kindness to lead as proper a life as possible under the circumstances. You would be surprised to know that most separated people are hoping and praying for just that kind of acceptance.

Leave the conversion to God. He will act in His own good time.

Since we chanced on the topic of God, perhaps it would be enlightening in concluding to look into the gospel and see how the author of the commandments dealt with the Samaritan woman, the lady caught in the act of adultery and Mary Magdalene.

GET THE STARS OUT OF YOUR EYES

She was 21 and the mother of two. He looked older than his 23 years and was single. They sought help because they loved each other and wanted to get married. But she already had a husband. However, after four stormy years, she honestly did not love him anymore. It was during one of their countless arguments that she met this sympathetic friend who eventually became her lover.

She complained that her husband spent most of his free time nightclubbing, day-clubbing, and "merienda-clubbing." He gambled a lot, too. And when he wasn't out with the boys, he stayed at home and drank heavily. Sometimes, he beat her. She said she had lost all her respect for him and wanted to get out of the house.

"Did he run around with his gang, and gamble and drink before you married him?" I asked.

"Yes," she replied, "but not so much."

"Then why did you marry him?" I insisted.

"Because he promised to change. Besides, I thought he would surely settle down when the children came," she said softly.

"Did he change?" I asked.

"No, he got worse. I now realize marrying him was such a terrible mistake," … and she wept.

How often have I engaged unhappy married couples in a similar dialogue? I have lost count. The tragedy, obviously, is that the horrible realization comes years too late. Too late for him, for her, and for the kids.

Whenever I attend a wedding, I look at the beautiful bride and the nervous groom and ask myself: "Are they going to be happy?" Will they eventually join the legions of separated people? Or will they experience just enough happiness to make life bearable? Or will they finally admit that they are remaining together 'for the sake of the kids"?

You must believe I am a terrible pessimist to think this way during a happy wedding. Perhaps it is because I am fully aware of the tremendous implications of that "I do." And because I have watched so many happy marriages go sour and end up on the rocks, I guess I have lost that romantic touch.

Don't get me wrong, I am not saying there are no happy marriages. I just don't think they are in the majority. You may not agree, but I still believe that countless marriages have been a disappointment. And you would be shocked to know how many spouses would not marry the same man/woman if they could only start all over again.

This is directed at our teenagers and to those of you who are still "searching." If you happen to be a married reader, then it's just too late for you. However, you can still dream, I suppose.

Too many women panic and fear they might end up spinsters if they are still single at twenty-five. In fact, the way they use the novena to Saint Jude and fall over any and all eligible men, I am convinced they are fishing blindly, hoping to land just about anybody. I get the impression almost any guy will do, so long as he can say "I do."

It was Saint Paul, I think, who said something about it being better to get married than to suffer the pains of hell. But I supposed it is better to stay single than to get married to someone who is a living hell and who makes life so miserable that the other hell doesn't look so forbidding anymore.

There are some things that I just don't understand. For instance … Why is it that a woman is so finicky and so fussy when it comes to selecting materials for a dress, and then hardly thinks twice about the selection of a man she swears she will live with till her dying days? Why is a man so very careful about choosing a career and so quick to ask a young woman, whom he has known only a few months, to stroll down the aisle and make a lifelong commitment? I suppose there are a number of reasons why people make the wrong choice.

However, I feel that haste, coupled with an overly "romantic" and unrealistic appraisal of the stringent demand of married life, are the root causes of bad selections.

Consequently, the thing to do is to try to keep your cool and control your heart so that it doesn't beat so loud that you can't hear yourself think. Remember, most people get just one shot at marriage. So calm down and take steady aim. If you miss your mark, it could mean separation, a life of tension, or just plain existence.

This is not meant to frighten or discourage. It is written in the hope that it might give rise to a few thoughts on the seriousness of this marriage business. Of course, much more could be said on the subject. However, I guess it all boils down to this: if you're looking for a partner in life, get the stars out of your eyes and look at where you are and where you're going.

PRAYER OF AN ENGAGED GIRL

Almighty God,
Thank you for bringing
my sweetheart into my life.

He's such a good guy
and I feel he is the
man for me.

But, Lord, I look around
and see so many broken
marriages. I don't
want mine to end up
a tragedy.

Lord, let me not be
blinded by the intense
feelings of love that
I have for this man.

Let my eyes see clearly
so that I may know
him well and make a
wise decision, so that,
In the years ahead.
we will, both of us,
have a full measure of
happiness.
Amen.

THE UGLY LITTLE WIFE

THIS IS THE STORY of Maribelle, the ugly little wife and her fight to keep her husband. Maribelle had met Victor four years before. After a seven-month courtship, the two married.

Maribelle had never fully understood why the dashing Victor had fallen for her in the first place. She was nothing much to look at and she knew it. There had been so many other beauties running after Vic that she could hardly believe her ears when he asked for her hand.

Victor, it must be said, was swept off his feet not at all by what Maribelle looked like but rather by what she was. "Belle," as he fondly liked to call her, had a sparkling personality. What made her even more compelling was the fact that she wasn't aware of it. Belle was also very intelligent and well read. She was an excellent conversationalist and a very efficient housewife who was always in complete control of her home. He enjoyed watching her moving around the house, softly instructing the maids about what to do. "It is so pleasant being with this woman," Vic often thought to himself. He knew that he could have had a prettier wife, but there was none as loving and as pleasant as Belle.

Vic worked in an office. He was an executive and moved around in a world of beautiful women. The temptations were many and varied. Belle understood this. She realized that competition of Vic's love and attention had not stopped with her walk to the altar. She was well aware that many unscrupulous women would not hesitate to give themselves to Vic, even if they know that he was married with two children. Belle had resolved, on her wedding day, to remain vigilant throughout her married life. She had promised herself never to let her guard down, never to take Vic for granted. She understood that if her husband was to remain faithful to her, he would need her help and active support.

For these reasons, Belle was always on the look-out for new ways and means to keep herself exciting for her husband. She did a lot of reading and shared with Vic what she had gathered from the books. She learned all about his job in the office and was genuinely interested in the business deals he was handling. At first, she had found it boring, but she stuck to it until she had cultivated an authentic interest. "If it's so important to Vic, if it's his life's work, I should know something about it and should be interested," she thought.

Belle was also a very neat dresser. She compensated for her lack of natural beauty by making frequent trips to the hairdresser. She was fully aware that Vic was surrounded daily by hordes of pretty girls who were more than pleasant to look at. She tried, as much as possible, to be always well kept in her husband's presence. She never came down for breakfast without first fixing her hair and putting on a touch of make-up and a pretty dress. Most wives, she knew, didn't bother, but they were a lot prettier too.

There were many times when Vic was tempted to stray and make left turns. But the thought of his wife and the happiness she afforded him were enough to keep him honest. People were amazed to see how happy both of them were and how kind life was to them.

Marriage is not an automatic gadget that functions well by itself with the push of a button. Both husband and wife have to work at it 24 hours a day. Perhaps if there were more ugly little women with the wisdom of a Maribelle, there would be far less unhappiness in married life.

END OF A MARRIAGE

THIS MORNING, I RECEIVED a very sad but touching letter from a reader. It told of the end of a marriage. I suppose the writer is in his thirties. For reasons that will be self-explanatory, I have decided to publish it in full because of the vital message contained therein.

Dear Bob:

This morning, my wife announced she is leaving me and our three children for good. Before this announcement, there were 11 years of marriage. To compress those years in a brief letter is obviously impossible. But I am writing some thoughts down, to reach through your column those who are just starting married life. Thus my heartbreak may prove of help.

These years have convinced me that nothing kills marital love more swiftly than an unbridled tongue.

When my wife walks through that door tomorrow, she will leave, besides a shattered home, a legacy of 11 years of bitter words. Within that span of time, she has charged me with practically all the faults on the books, plus a few hefty sins thrown in for good measure.

Her tongue-lashing has been liberally administered in the privacy of our bedroom, before our children, in the presence of maids, to the faces of relatives, before visitors, and even in the office.

When her temper cools, she explains with a tongue once more under control that all these were acts of virtue. "Frankness and candor require the tongue-lashings," she says in all sincerity.

I do not question her motives, although I do not agree with her judgment. And one tries to forgive, since that is the duty of one who aspires to be called a Christian.

To my dying day, there is one incident I will always remember after my five-year-old son witnessed his mother tongue-lash me for a fault I cannot even remember. This boy slipped in quietly while I was shaving and said in all the God-given simplicity of childhood:

"Papa huwag mo nalang sabihin kay Mama pero naaawa ako sa iyo." (Papa just don't tell Mama, but I sympathize with you.)

There are many things that make for marital peace. But could you tell the young couples that you reach through the Chronicle column: "a tight leash on the tongue is one that makes for happiness, especially for the young children that God may see fit to entrust to your care."

(Name withheld)

Everybody has a breaking point. Two people can shout at one another for a while, patch things up and still keep their marriage in one piece. If this "fight-reconciliation-fight" situation is allowed to continue, it is only a matter of time before distrust sets in and things take a turn for the worse.

How long can the "for the sake of the children" argument keep them together, is not known. Some people can take more punishment than others. But few can take it forever. Sooner or later, there will be resentment and the inevitable ensuing explosion and a lot of irreparable hurt feelings. For this reason, it is of paramount importance that the root cause of the "same old arguments" be eliminated as quickly as possible.

Marital disagreements are to be expected. However, the frustrations that emerge due to repeated unresolved crises have proven over a period of time to be deadly.

I feel sorry for our letter writer. His marriage is a tragedy that can be a lesson to all of us. However, I am hardly surprised. Eleven years of suffering is a long time.

WHY MAN HAS TO BE FIRST

Ever since the beginning of the history of man, woman has always been a second-rate citizen. Not just in government and in other fields of endeavor, but even in her own little domain—the home.

Woman has always been treated in an inferior way by man. He has bought her and sold her like cattle. She has been kept in harems, executed for adultery (the man always got away) used for man's pleasure, and generally reduced to the state of slavery. She has been banished from the halls of parliament and refused the right to vote. She has had to submit to the "double standard." In short, she has been completely subjugated by man who has given her attention when he has deemed it proper and neglected her otherwise. Even today, in the space age, woman is still denied the right to go to the polls in some "civilized" countries, hold certain jobs, and in general stand on an equal footing with man.

There seems to be only one fundamental reason for her plight—her inferior physical make-up. Man has pushed her around because of his brute strength. She has had to use finesse and other sly techniques to offset this disadvantage and to survive physically and emotionally.

In addition to his physical superiority, man has held down woman because of a strong need to keep an exaggerated self-image and the closeness with which this image is tied, to his sexuality.

Man is always accusing woman of being vain. He laughs at her meticulousness in the selection of clothing and the fixing of her hair. What man hardly realizes and will almost always deny publicly is the *fact* that he is at least as vain as woman. However, his is a different type of vanity. It usually has something to do with his physical attributes and his sexuality.

He relishes sports. The tougher, the better. Excellence in the field of athletics is generally a much sought after honor. Bravery and courage in battle have always been and still are just about the greatest proof of manhood recognized the world over.

Just as important, however, is the sexual prowess of man. The greatest warrior would be laughed at and scorned by most men if he were found to be impotent or afraid of going to bed with a woman. Even in Philippine society, there is still the prevalent belief among most men that the more women a man has had, the more virile he must be.

These factors have almost forced man to keep woman in second place. He has always felt that should woman step ahead of him, even for one moment, he would be less a man. Most women have understood this and have allowed their men to take the lead. They have not wished to chance wounding man's vanity and have consequently remained quietly in the background. Those women who have not understood this and have stepped on men's feet to get where they are can testify to the scorn and, at times, the outright hostility of the opposite sex. No man likes to be outdone by a woman; no male wants to admit that a woman is better than he, even if she is. It may not be fair, but right now, that's the way things stand.

THE SEXUAL MALE

How a man functions depends, to a great extent, on his self-image. And much of man's self-image is based upon his ability to perform sexually. Biologically, sexual intercourse demands active participation on the part of the male. Woman may be physically passive, but not man. Man has no choice.

Man enjoys his role as the instigator because this assures protection for his self-image. As the aggressor, he initiates sexual activity only when he is reasonably sure of his ability to perform successfully. If there is any doubt, he can always postpone any action until a future time. And woman is supposed to lie back and wait for him to decide the date and time.

Successful sexual participation is so important to the male that any doubts about it will surely make of him a miserable creature. In order to reassure themselves of their sexual prowess, many middle-aged men will begin to wander and play around. And usually they chase after young and inexperienced girls.

Whenever a distraught wife comes to me complaining that her husband is having an affair after 20 years of marriage, she is amazed to find that I can almost always guess the age of the mistress.

The reason an older man picks on a young girl is that she is less apt to be qualified to judge him sexually. He then becomes clearly superior to her. A woman his own age could be a startling beauty, but the man who doubts his sexual abilities will want to have nothing to do with her since she could become an excellent judge of his diminishing sexual powers.

Another reason an older man will run after a much younger woman is that he is sure to overwhelm her in all or most aspects. He is more knowledgeable about the world, business, people, etc. He knows his way around and the little girl is 'wowed' by his seeming sureness about everything. This superiority over woman is an important reassurance to a man beset with gnawing doubts about his manhood.

Of course, men will vehemently deny what I have just written until they are blue in the face.

Doctors tell us that the male reaches the peak of his sexual powers during his late teens. Woman, on the other hand, reaches a comparable height in her late twenties. The fact is that a 30-year old woman may demand a lot more of a man of the same age than the latter can give.

It is not surprising then that man has tried (and succeeded) in down-grading woman's role in sex. He has always maintained the image of superiority in the realm of sexuality. The truth is that he has created for himself an illusory world wherein he has made himself king.

Woman has, on the other hand, played his game. She has allowed him to use her as an instrument of pleasure. She has permitted him to think himself superior (and consequently better) to her. In short, she has contributed to his exaggerated self-image, which he finds so necessary to succeed.

It would be wise for a woman who loves her husband not to challenge him too strongly in this field. This is one occasion when coming out second best means a clear-cut victory.

PEACE

BUDDY IS A MARRIED MAN with four children. Six years of living with Melva have brought about many significant changes in his personality and lifestyle. At 32, Buddy has become a very serious person. Some of his friends say that he has lost his zest for life. Others say that marriage has not been good to him.

In fact, Buddy has become a bitter and disillusioned person. Often, he catches himself thinking of the "old days" when he courted his pretty office-mate, Melva. How he found her so lovely and so exciting and so full of life! He often remembers how he fell head over heels in love with her and how they enjoyed each other's presence.

Their marriage started off on the right foot. They were close-and very much in love. Their first child (a boy) came along and added to their joy. Then there was the second—a girl this time. More joy.

What neither one of them really noticed was the way few seemingly insignificant differences began to establish themselves as patterns in their lives. Regularly, the same irritating arguments would surface. There would be some impatience. Then Melva was sure to raise her voice. Then, after controlling for some time, Buddy would shout her down. The argument ended when Melva would sit down and bury her face in her hands and cry.

Time and time again, the two made up, only to have the same gnawing incident repeat themselves over and over again. Buddy loved his wife. Melva had her moments of jealousy and doubts despite his faithfulness. This often angered him and caused tension and conflict between them.

However, what seemed to trouble and tire Buddy more than anything else was their seeming inability to solve those nagging and recurring arguments.

Buddy was tired. Tired of the same arguments and the same conclusions that neither one of them could understand and accept. He felt as though he was always running into a stone wall. And it looked like the wall was six meters thick.

It had come to a point where Buddy suddenly realized that he longed to delay coming home in the evening. He also caught himself wishing to avoid Melva. And, there were times when he felt so frustrated and tired of the "same old fights" that he even felt repulsed by the idea of making love to his pretty wife.

Melva seemed not to get the same message. Of course, she did not enjoy the conflicts either. Perhaps she got so upset that she just could not help it. She could find no way to resolve the difficulties.

Buddy and Melva are typical of many married couples. Even among young people courting (and friends too) their situation is not unusual.

Surely one of the greatest frustrations in a man's life is his inability to resolve a recurring problem with a loved one. And what is the worse is that, when it comes to dealing with frustrations, everybody has a breaking point. It is not rare to see friends and married people allow a similar situation to deteriorate to such an extent that the love between them is suffocated by the tension and slowly withers and dies.

What is needed, if the conflicts cannot immediately be resolved, is a period of relative peace wherein their battered love may be given enough of that emotional fresh air and sunshine that is so vital.

A man can weather a storm-but not forever. A soldier can fight long and hard and bravely, but even he needs rest. A husband (and a wife too) can bear tension for quite some time, but not indefinitely. Sometimes, what is needed is peace. Given enough of it, it is amazing how many insignificant problems and difficulties melt away into nothingness.

GROWING UP IN EVERY WAY

FROM THE TIME HE is born, man is supposed to grow physically, spiritually, emotionally, and socially. He needs food for his body, nourishment for his soul, and he needs friends to develop into an emotionally well-balanced social being.

And when the time comes in the lives of most people to choose a companion to live with for life, these various processes of growth should continue. I feel sorry for many of the married people I meet. They are very unhappy and often just existing and not really living. Because of the intense marital conflicts, continuous struggles and the resultant alienation, countless married people have stopped growing. Many have even regressed.

It is therefore of prime importance that young people (and the older ones too) understand not only themselves but their marriage. It is good for them to know what to expect in the coming years.

Psychologists specializing in marriage relationships usually speak of three different phases in married life. The first is the "honeymoon phase." The couple feels that they really and truly understand each other so well that is almost too good to be true. They find it amazingly unusual. They like the same things; they agree in almost all matters; they are able to talk things over between themselves; they can often read one another's thoughts; they sense each other's feelings. In short, during the honeymoon phase, which can last for as long as a few years, husband and wife still have the sense of spontaneous mutual understanding and sameness.

By nature, we invariably choose mates who are complementary to ourselves. We discover in our partners those qualities and assets that we always looked for and desired intensely since adolescence. The first phase is usually characterized by a wonderful sense of completeness.

According to some experts, the second phase ordinarily comes between the fifth and the tenth years. During this time, the slow realization that both are not what each one thought the other to be, begins to creep into the minds of the couple. They slowly discover faults that for many months had lain unnoticed deep beneath the surface. Other defects that both had thought would be corrected in the time by their great mutual love aggravate things and make life more and more difficult.

The faults can be sometimes quite significant and very destructive. She is very moody. He shows a violent streak when drunk. She lies. He's very selfish.

At first, they begin by warning each other. Then they plead, scold, and end up hating the day they said "I do" at the foot of the altar. All of a sudden, nobody understands anybody anymore.

At this point (the third phase), one of two things can happen. Either one of the parties can withdraw and give up the field to the other and progressively abandon the fight for happiness, or both of them can make an attempt to iron out things and accept one another and find a modus vivendi. The first option means certain disaster since it is usually only a question of time before the one being crushed gets tired of being stepped on and rebels. When this happens, everything explodes. The result is either separation or a life of unending conflict.

The wisest choice is the second. To accept one's partner and recognize him for what he is, divested of all the fabrications for the mind and the imagination. It becomes a matter of facing reality rather than running away from it.

Perhaps the description of a similar situation by a noted psychiatrist could best illustrate my point.

"Indeed, he has faults: he has problems which he has not succeeded in solving. He does not understand himself and he reacts most distastefully when his faults are pointed out. He reacts in this way precisely because he does not feel capable of overcoming his faults. But he can be helped in a quite different fashion: simply by loving him, not so much for his qualities as for his problems. He can be helped simply by understanding what he missed in his childhood years and what he is still missing, and by seeking to fill that need."

It isn't easy to live a happy married life. But then, nobody ever said it was all that simple.

PREDICTING THE UNPREDICTABLE

The young husband was obviously very frustrated. He sat back in his chair and, with arms outstretched in apparent despair, whispered to me: "Bob, it's no use. We just don't think alike."

How often have I heard the same words from tired and puzzled spouses? What most of us fail to realize is that we were not created alike by the Almighty. The Bible says that He created them male and female. So many are blinded by the obvious physical differences between man and woman that they are unaware of the deeper underlying complexities of the male and the female.

Any husband who expects his wife to think the way he does is in for a very big surprise. And the wife who is waiting for her husband to change his thinking is going to wait a very long time indeed.

The tragedy of it all is that, after many years of living together, a man and a woman can understand one so poorly. I think many heartaches could be avoided if both spouses stopped for a while to study the inborn factors that largely contribute to conflict and tension in the home.

Since time immemorial, countless young husbands have attempted to understand the seemingly irrational and unpredictable behavior of their wives. What they usually notice is the unexplainable changes in the wife's mood.

"Yesterday," a man said to me, "I told my wife she is pretty and she smiled. Today, I told her the same thing and she broke down and cried. I just don't know what to make of her anymore."

When this happens, it may be that some biological condition is causing her to react in such a way. Perhaps it would be a good idea for the husband to sit down with his wife and her calendar and try to discover the pattern with her monthly menstrual cycle. If the man does this, he will ordinarily find a distinct relationship. Often, knowing the relationship between personality changes and menstrual cycle is all that is needed to help them live together more comfortably. The husband is aware and is expecting some difficult situations at certain predictable times. This makes it easier for him to dismiss her seemingly arbitrary moods with a smile and a word of kindness. Men do not suffer the inconvenience and physical suffering that women bear as a matter of fact. Males find it hard to understand how much physical discomfort a woman feels as she goes about her daily chores.

If a man does not comprehend the biological factors that play a part in the behavior of a woman, he will no doubt attempt to reform her and change the unchangeable. If he understands that some of her moodiness is because of her biological make-up, he is more apt to relax and accept it all as one of the differences between a man and woman.

A woman spends one week preparing physically for menstruation, a week having it, and another week getting over it. That means the three out of four weeks every month will not be normal. This purely biological factor accounts for the generally greater intensity of the woman's moods when compared to the man's and must be considered when the male attempts to relate to the female. Doctors tell us that usually "the period just before menstruation begins is one of tension, irritability, and depression."

If every husband (and sweetheart too) can remember this simple physical phenomenon, he will find his wife a lot easier to live with. He may even come to a point where he will enjoy predicting with accuracy her unpredictability.

THE MANY LOVES OF DELIA

SHE HAD HER FIRST BOYFRIEND at 13. Her second, six months later. Her third, shortly after she turned 14. By the time Delia had reached the age of 19, she had more than her share of sweethearts.

However, it seems that the pattern was the same in her relationship with all the guys in her life. She was easily attracted to men and quick to fall in love with them. Her love was equally superficial and of short duration. Even though she did not know a guy very well, she had very often gotten involved sexually.

Now a woman of 22 years, Delia went on with her whirlwind affair. She lost her virginity long ago and was classified in the language of the men who knew her as "easy."

It was not that Delia was a cheap girl because she was not. It was just Delia could not seem to be able to cultivate a deep friendship and make it work for any substantial length of time. Things never seemed to work out for her. Every time she had a new suitor, her heart would bubble over with enthusiasm. "This time," she would think to herself, "it's going to be different," But it never seemed to be "different." The affair would end like the others had before. Parties, movies, sweet words, promises, sexual involvement, boredom, and finally separation. Delia could not understand it. She would, with all her heart, try to be sincere, but things never seemed to work out.

There are many young women like Delia. No matter how hard they try, they never seem to succeed in love. Perhaps it's because they are too much in a hurry to fall in love. Perhaps they do not realize that before there is authentic love, there must be deep friendship. And friendship doesn't just happen. It must be worked at … and worked at hard.

I remember a meaningful song I enjoy listening to. It speaks of a beautiful friendship between a man and a woman. It tells how they treated one another as brother and sister. It recounts how they did things together and just simply enjoyed one another's company. And it described how one evening both of them understood that this was the end of a beautiful friendship and the beginning of love.

What Delia and girls like her do not understand is that serious men look for more in a girl than just fun. What they fail to comprehend is that men, whether they be mature or not, easily get bored with women. Unless there is more to their affair than partying and movie-going and just having fun, there can be no lasting relationship of any worth.

Unless Delia comes to the realization that love is an art that is not easily mastered, she will go on and on looking for an easy romance. She will forever be searching for that satisfying love that will always elude her. She will, again and again, believe that with each new relationship, she has finally come to the end on her quest. And after repeated failures and disillusionments, she will grow weary and finally succumb to discouragement. She may even give up her desire for a deep and lasting love and settle for whatever momentary pleasure a superficial relationship may bring. When that day dawns, Delia will begin to walk the long downhill path of despair. And unless someone reaches out to her in authentic and sincere friendship, she may never find her way back.

FOR MARRIED COUPLES ONLY

YOU MAY ASK YOURSELVES, what right do I have to write about the topic I intend to develop today. In fact, I myself have hesitated for quite some time before gathering up enough courage to put some of these thoughts down on paper.

After some time, I decided to go ahead anyway, even at the risk of being misunderstood. I am sure some people will think I am imprudent, rude, and perhaps even unkind. Never mind, I believe much unhappiness and suffering can be avoided if only a married couple understood more fully what I want to say.

Before going on, it is important that you know the sources of my information: actual experiences of married men and women as related to me and a lot of reading. I have put all of this together, thought about it, and here you have it.

During the course of my many conversations with unhappy married women, I have had the opportunity to listen to a long list of things that make a woman miserable. It often happens that the wife will say to me in a quiet, subdued manner: "… and, Bob, whenever he makes love to me, I don't enjoy it at all. I get the feeling that all he wants is his own pleasure. He never thinks of me."

Countless women have the same feeling. The way men sometimes take their wives to bed makes me wonder if we should not create a new expression to describe the reality of what's happening. Perhaps we could call it "qualified rape."

The word rape is usually defined as the seizure and carnal knowledge of a woman against her will. The way I get it from so many wives, it looks like some of the goings-on in the bedroom come pretty close to fulfilling that definition. However, considering that both have a legal right over each other's body, I suppose I would have to qualify the word "rape," even if the woman does not wish to have sexual intercourse.

It is amazing how many women submit to their husbands when, in fact, they have no desire to do so. It is not uncommon for a female to feel deep revulsion at the simple prospect of being sexually intimate with the man she has vowed to love forever.

Perhaps it is because she no longer loves him that she feels this way. When a woman goes to bed with a man she does not love, she feels she is merely being used to promote the sexual pleasure of the man. She may not love him one bit, as in the case of the prostitute. Or, she may no longer love her husband. Or, she may love him dearly, but feel he does not love or care for her anymore.

In all three instances, the woman feels she is a tool. She remains, deep in her heart, very miserable. She experiences a great emptiness. She feels cheated and dirty. And she begins to believe that sex is filthy and ugly.

Let's talk about the man and woman who are really and truly in love. It may also happen that the male may sincerely try to please his wife but offends her unknowingly, anyway.

I once met a young woman who told me: "Bob, my husband thinks that he is such a great lover. But he doesn't know that, during our seven years of marriage, he has never pleased me sexually."

Intercourse, for a man, is something to do. For a woman, it is something to experience. Men are too often tough—even brutal—in their method. They feel this is how a real man should approach a woman. The female, at least until she is repeatedly disillusioned, desires tenderness, warmth, affection and communication. She expects more than a physical union. Sex without communicating love is meaningless and damnable.

A woman is deeply hurt when, immediately after experiencing his pleasure, her husband rolls over and turns his back on her and goes to sleep. A happily married woman once told me; "My husband is so very thoughtful. He always waits for me."

Men should keep in mind the counsels of medical people who advise husbands to show care by speaking tender, loving words during the act of love. Husbands should be careful to prove to their wives that sexual pleasure is of secondary importance.

The most tender and memorable moments in the lives of married people can occur during this intimate physical act. However, if there is no love, no consideration, no care, what was meant by God to be beautiful and attractive can become ugly and repulsive.

MARITAL HELL

LILIAN IS A PRETTY mother of three. After five years of "marriage" (quotation hers), this young woman of 33 is ready to abandon ship.

"Five years of hell is a long time," she says. Indeed, it is.

It all started very early. Their courtship was superficial, lacking in depth and perception. Lilian was enthralled by the apparent charm of Gary. He had struck her as being a mature and solid man, and so, in a flash, she had fallen hard for him.

Gary had also been swept off his feet by his wife's beauty and personality. It had all been too much of a whirlwind courtship. When they married, they suddenly discovered that they were strangers in their own house.

Gary and Lilian were both nice people, but they were never meant to live together in marital bliss. As it often happens, this was a case of two wonderful people who just did not click well together. Their marriage, which was meant to be an opportunity for self-fulfillment and happiness, had become a veritable trap with no apparent way out.

As a marriage counselor, I am a witness to the terrible agonies that married people in such a situation must bear. I marvel at the patience and the enduring emotional and psychological strength of some of these men and women caught up in this web of circumstances.

They live under the same roof for years, grappling and wrestling with one another. They are always tense and forever arguing over the same old differences. And when you stop and study the reasons for their daily battles, you will find that there is nothing very serious in the first place. It is usually just plain incompatibility.

I really believe that if I were in their shoes, I would simply walk away. Not even for the sake of the children would I keep such a union together. Please don't get shocked! I am not advocating divorce. I *am* saying that I don't see the point in two people being forced to live together when they are forever at each other's throat.

I am a firm believer in the line of a popular song that says: "A house is not a home when there's no one there to hold you tight, no one there you can kiss goodnight." Some people think that a husband and wife should be kept together at any price. I cannot agree. I think that sometimes the price is too high.

"For the sake of the children." Yes, "the children." The children of such marriages are witnesses to the daily fights and the pettiness of their parents. They learn to live in an atmosphere of tension and insecurity. They learn hatred. They feel obliged to take sides when they love both Mom and Dad.

Far too many people think that when a husband and wife are living together with their kids under the same roof, there you have a family. I don't think so. I would venture to say that many of these so called "families" are mere groupings of people who, because of an accident of birth and pure circumstances, happen to eat and sleep in the same house.

There is no true family unless there is real communication and authentic interaction that is sealed with plenty of deep love. Anything less does not, I think, constitute a family.

Children are far better off living with one of their parents peacefully rather than staying with a mother and father who are not in love with each other. Growing up in a family where the parents are separated is, of course, not a good thing. But sometimes it is the lesser of two evils.

When two people are hopelessly at odds with each other, when they have tried everything to save their marriage and failed, when they are miserable almost all the time, then, I say, *break it up* before bitter hatred and crippling despair move into the lives of the unhappy spouses. Even the Catholic Church is not against separation (separation is not divorce). It recognizes that every couple has a breaking point.

Besides, life is too short to live in marital hell.

DIVORCE, A POOR SUBSTITUTE

BILLY AND NENA HAVE BEEN married seven years now. They have three children and the fourth is on the way. Everyone thinks that this couple is very happy indeed. The fact is, however, that not only are Billy and Nena unhappy, they are ready to separate.

Unknown to their friends, they have been fighting and quarreling and finally hating each other to such a point that life has become unbearable for them. Both would very much want to finish with their marriage. However, here in the Philippines, divorce is not allowed. Even if it were, it would not matter much because Billy and Nena are Roman Catholics.

There has been a lot of talk lately about the pros and cons of a divorce law here in the country. People have asked me what I think of it. To tell you the truth, I couldn't care less. Whether or not divorce is allowed, it is not really going to change anything.

Those who think that they would be happier with the option to re-marry always before them are sorely mistaken. In the United States, we have loads of divorced people who have failed once, twice, or more and are still unhappy. What I'm trying to say is that divorce is a poor substitute for maturity and good sense.

I don't really care whether or not the government enacts a divorce law. It's not going to affect the teaching of the Church. Even if the State allows it, the Church won't. So the law will be there, but Catholics will not be allowed to make use of it. On the other hand, it may be that if divorce is permitted in this country, it will be possible to fix a lot of messy marriages that, up to now, the Church has not been able to touch.

Take, for instance, the cases of the countless young people who rush into marriage before a justice of peace and shortly after break up without having had a Catholic wedding. They could get a divorce and marry in the Church. Or the case of a Catholic couple that is granted an annulment by the Church. When the two separate and given permission by the Church to re-marry, they can't do so now because their marriage is still binding in the eyes of the State. Divorce could rectify that.

There is, of course, the other side of the coin. Many immature couples could use divorce as an escape hatch from their responsibilities. Things could get quite messy if countless people kept swapping partners. This is what many anti-divorce people are saying will undoubtedly happen.

Well, after having spent 28 years in this country closely observing what is going on in homes and marriages, I think I can safely say that the swapping, the infidelity, the queridas abound. I suppose all that divorce would do would be to make the querida system illegal in the eyes of the State. As far as the Church is concerned, nothing would change.

You and I all know that there are plenty of people who have a "Number Two." Some adept individuals go so far as having a "Number Three" and a "Number Four." And they usually get away with it too.

Often, the poor wife is helpless because she is not protected under the law. Oh yes, she could bring adultery proceedings against her husband, but you know what that means. So perhaps a man would think twice about fooling around if he knew that his wife could divorce him.

I am not advocating divorce. I am not saying also that we should not have it. I'm simply stating that as far as the Church is concerned, it would not make one hit of difference.

What I am saying is that there is more to a successful marriage than a piece of paper. What I am saying is that perhaps there should be a law limiting marriage to mature people. Perhaps people should undergo psychological testing before being allowed to take out a marriage license. What I am saying is that if people were more careful in getting married, there would be hardly any need to see them "unmarried."

Sooner or later I think divorce will be allowed by the State. However, I'll be dead a long time before the Church allows it. As long as people think that divorce is a cure-all and that it is the answer to their problems, then I don't see how it's going to change anything.

I'm sure that many people will understand what I've written. I expect it. I'm certain that some will say that I'm in favor of divorce. Others will say I'm not. The truth is, as I've said before, one way or the other, I really don't care.

WORKING WIVES

ONE PROBLEM THAT COMES up quite often in my counseling is that of the married woman who wants very much to work and whose husband is equally adamant in keeping her at home. At first glance, the difficulty does not seem to be of earthshaking importance. However, if you dig deeper into the heart of the matter, you will find that there is more than meets the eye.

Why does a wife want to work in the first place? Well, in a country where maids do most of the hard housework, the average city housewife does not have enough things to do in the home to keep her busy. So, to escape boredom and/or to supplement the husband's income, she desires to work.

If her husband permits her, she can expect to begin a whole series of adjustments to cope with the new situation. First, there is the schedule. The working wife may leave the house before the husband and perhaps come home later. And, depending on her job, she may have plenty of overtime, etc., etc.

Some men are not willing to allow their wives to get a job. I have seen husbands prefer to do without a better material life rather than allow the wife to go work. Why?

I think one of the most common reasons is that fear men harbor in their hearts. They believe that a job will provide their wives with the temptation for extra-marital experimentation. Every observant husband knows that the working wife tends to compare her husband to the men she sees around her. This man earns more than her hubby. That one has a more pleasant personality. Her co-worker is better looking. Besides, he seems to care so much about her and certainly understands her more.

How many husbands can stand that kind of comparison? Countless men would rather not run the risk of playing second fiddle to a smart company executive. So, the logical conclusion is to keep the wife at home where she can be isolated from the wolf packs that prey on working girls (married and single).

Men have been comparing their wives to their pretty secretaries for years. It's unfair, but they have been doing it all along. However, when both she and he are doing it, the trouble is compounded. Both become extremely critical of each other. Arguments and quarrels arise and tension begins to undermine their relationship.

He starts to nag her about quitting her job. Since she has tasted freedom from the boredom of dreary housework, she finds it distasteful to return to the four walls of her home.

Besides, now that she is working, she feels less dependent financially on her husband (she may even be earning more). She knows that if anything happens between them, she can support herself. She has her own income and can leave when she wishes. (I know of many women who would separate if only they could feed themselves.)

Unlike the barrio woman who is completely dependent financially on her husband, the working wife does not really need her husband in the economic sense of the word. Therefore, separation is easier for her to contemplate.

In this column, I have dwelt only on the situation of working wives and have purposely omitted to discuss the working mother, which will be the subject of another article.

Am I in favor of working wives? It depends. Each case should be dealt with individually. Today, I merely wanted to point out some of the advantages and drawbacks involved.

LOVE AND UNDERSTANDING

MARIE IS 23 YEARS OLD and is madly in love with Eddie, a young junior executive. They have been courting for six months and are now contemplating a June wedding.

Ask Marie why she is walking on a cloud most of the time and she will tell you that it is because she has never in her life met such an understanding and loving person as Eddie. She will tell you that there are no secrets between them. Anything that comes to her mind, no matter how seemingly insignificant, is related to her beloved.

Our two lovers are so happy and contented that they are living in an almost unreal world. The reason for their boundless joy and exhilaration is, of course, that they love and understand each other.

However, so many people have heard this said and have seen it written, but do not really grasp the deep meaning of this truth.

Love and understanding are so closely linked that it is just about impossible to find where one ends and the other begins. It is also not known, I think, if love causes understanding or if understanding causes love. The man who understands, loves, and the woman who loves, understands. If you feel understood, you feel loved; and if you feel loved, you feel sure you are understood. Both love and understanding are as one.

I suppose it is this way because a man needs to feel deeply loved in order to risk sharing himself and the intimate secrets that have made his life what it is. He will never dare reveal certain inner thoughts and aspirations to anybody—except perhaps to that one special person who loves him above all else, and in loving him thus, accepts him for what he is.

For this reason, he is not afraid of opening his heart, for he knows he will not be laughed at and ridiculed. He does not fear to tell of his high aspirations and his "impossible dream" because he knows that if he talks like the great person he would want to be, his loved one will give him an understanding smile.

If a man can do this, he will suddenly find himself pouring out more and more of himself to the one he trusts. And he is moving ever closer to this "special person." Obviously, this is because the new found confidant is the keeper of so many secrets.

However, this kind of sharing is overwhelming and very rare. There are countless fears that prevent us from opening up. We fear showing too much emotion. We are also afraid that we may not be taken seriously. How many people come to me and before uttering even one word, begin to cry and then say: "I'm sorry, Bob." (Sorry for what?) How many tell me, almost apologetically, that their problems are not very big. (As if I won't listen unless they are of earth-shaking importance.)

Perhaps the reason for these fears is that people have been burned on account of them before. And the burns were extremely painful and have left many ugly scars.

How often have I seen men and women broken up and driven into horrible isolation because somebody they trusted and thought would understand them was a disappointment? By the time they come to me, there are only two things left for me to do: listen and care. If I can do this sincerely, well, then I will have helped restore their trust and confidence in people and given them the courage to risk opening up their hearts again.

I guess the reason there is so much suffering and war in the world is that nations are very much like people—they don't listen and they don't trust.

IS IT TOO LATE FOR ERNESTO AND FELY?

ERNESTO AND FELY HAVE been married for nine years. They have three children, two boys and a girl. They are wealthy. They live in a big house. They both came from "good" families. Ernesto and Fely have another thing in common. They are both unhappy. In fact, "miserable" might be the better world.

Almost from the very beginning, things went wrong. First there was his gambling and drinking that upset her. She started to nag him about it. He resented her. Then she left home and went back to her Mama. He felt deeply hurt and very embarrassed. She came back, but only after a lot of unpleasantness and more hurt feelings.

There followed a whole series of arguments and misunderstandings. Things got to a point where hardly a day passed without some conflict between them. The tension became so great that even a drive into the country on a Sunday afternoon was risky business. They always seemed to find something to argue about. Perhaps it was because they were falling out of love. And when you do not love a person anymore, you become intolerant and impatient.

At any rate, things got so hot that both of them preferred being with somebody else. Ernesto would stay out a lot later than usual, while Fely took up mahjong and spent more time at the gambling table than anywhere else. The wife was not surprised when she heard rumors that her husband was carrying on an affair with a hostess.

It was only at this late stage that somebody suggested that both of them see a counsellor. The man they called upon was wise and experienced and it did not take him long to see that this marriage was in critical condition. He knew that both husband and wife would have to go a long way to save their marriage. Deep in his heart, he doubted whether there was enough love left between them to bring about the change.

As things worked out, his misgiving was well founded. Neither Ernesto nor Fely were willing to make the necessary adjustments. Their marriage was spinning out of control and they knew it. However, rebuilding a relationship, putting the pieces back together again is not an easy task. And when there is little or no love left, it becomes an impossible dream.

Perhaps it was with some relief that the unhappy couple heard the advice of the counsellor. "I think you had better separate," he said solemnly.

The above story is not unusual. Everyday people admit that their marriage has failed and give up on each other. Perhaps it is good that they do so. Prolonging a miserable situation in life that has become unbearable makes no sense. Even the Church allows separation. (I did not say divorce.)

Ernesto and Fely, and others like them, usually pass up their only chances of reversing what seems to be inevitable and drift away from one another. As a counselor, I have seen one thing they all have in common. They have all waited too long to seek help.

When they get to the counselor, the marriage is in critical condition. In most instances, it is not a question of fixing a relationship but rebuilding a friendship and starting from the bottom up. This is not at all easy. It takes almost super-human willpower to overlook all the hurt that was caused in the past and to try to see the other party in a new light.

Some people have said that an unhappy marriage is a disease. I suppose that in some ways it is. If you do not catch the sickness in its initial stages, then you can be sure that the cure will not be easy. It may even happen that the best doctors and the latest medical facilities will not be enough. Likewise, if a marriage has gone too far downhill, the road back may be so difficult and so long that the possibility of reconciliation is extremely remote.

If you have a friend or loved one who is having a marital problem that is in the slightest was becoming serious, the best you can do for him is to convince him to move before it is too late. And if you who are reading this happen to be one of those concerned, then my advice to you can be summarized in two words: MOVE NOW!

TO TOUCH OR NOT TO TOUCH

THE LITTLE TEENAGER WAS sitting alone in my office when I came in. I knew right away that something serious was troubling her. Her stiff posture and downcast eyes, the tension around her mouth and the way she played nervously with the pink tissue on her lap, all told me that this sixteen-year-old had a big problem.

"Hi there! How's everything?"

I sat down and leaned forward, trying to look into those sad eyes of hers that did their best to avoid me.

"What's wrong?" I asked.

She looked away silently. Still, I could see the tears welling up in her eyes. She had been deeply hurt. That was obvious. And she had come to me to open her heart and unburden herself because she believed I could help. But she could not be sure about how I would receive her. Would I be impatient with her? Would I get irritated? Would I hate her and reject her if she told me all? Would I get shocked and distressed because of what she wanted to tell me?

I knew these questions were racing through her mind. She wanted some kind of sign, a reassurance that she could and should trust me, and that I really and truly cared. I gave it to her.

I reached out and touched her hand. She did not look up. Then, I took it in mine. "Hey, your hand is cold," I remarked. A little smile appeared on her lips, but she continued to look down and away.

"Hey, little sister, look at me; look into my eyes." She did. "Do I hate you? I know you've got a big problem. Tell me about it. I want to help." I smiled, and at the same time I squeezed her hand tightly.

Then it happened. A flood of tears fell from her eyes. They were tears of relief. She knew where I stood. She could trust me now. She wept. And after using up two or three tissues (I always keep a couple of boxes handy) she told me all.

It is amazing what a simple touch can do to a person. I wanted her to trust me, so I held her hand because I realized that she knew, even only subconsciously, that this is a sign of caring. Your enemy does not hold your hand when you're sad. I was also sure that this simple touch would trigger off the tears. And she needed to cry to relieve the tension and the pain within.

In our very conservative society, we have been taught the "no touch system." It's too bad, because it's sad. We miss out on so much because we don't know how to touch another person.

We have the impression that to touch is "sinful" and that it is "disrespectful" and impure. Perhaps it is because our minds are so filthy that we cannot imagine a man touching another person (man or woman) without suspecting some foul play.

We have been taught that to touch another person, especially someone of the opposite sex, is so improper that we have come to a point where we believe that just about all kinds and types of touch are forbidden.

Oh, I understand some of the objections you might have in mind. I have thought about them too—and dismissed most of them as not valid.

When a baby is born, doctors strongly advise the mother to hold and cuddle it as much and as often as possible. Everybody, to a greater or lesser degree, is aware of the fact that the infant needs this physical contact if he is to feel the security he craves for so desperately. Ever noticed how a child stops crying when his mother scoops him up into her arms and hugs him tightly? It is the touch that conveys the message that "all will be well, because I'll protect you from harm."

We have forgotten that it was not so very long ago that we were children and in great need of this type of reassurance. We have even thought ourselves so strong and self-sufficient that we feel we no longer need the support of a hand on the shoulder.

It is only when we start going to pieces that we see and feel the need to hold a person. We have all viewed the "touching" photographs of wounded soldiers literally lying in the arms of their comrades.

I have held grown men in my arms as they wept on my shoulder following the loss of loved one. One of the girls in the Arcilla hostage incident rushed into my arms and hugged me tightly when I walked into the room where they were being held at gunpoint. I am sure she felt a certain sense of security, there in my arms, for the first time in many hours.

A THING OF BEAUTY

THEY SAY THAT BEAUTY is only "skin deep." True ... so true. It is also true that many women forget that it is so—especially when they are still teenagers. The older a woman gets, the more she realizes that there are values that are more than just "skin deep."

Men, however, have to make a constant effort to remind themselves that the physical beauty in a woman is indeed fleeting. Men are so easily and quickly drawn to "skin deep" that they very often lose perspective when it comes to loving.

Many an older married man has hurt his faithful wife by comparing her directly and/or indirectly to a Binibining Pilipinas. Women know that physical beauty rates highly with men—the thinking and the unthinking ones. They remember that they used their physical attributes to lure their men closer to themselves. And whenever they see their husband eyeing a beautiful girl (even though she may be a complete stranger) most wives feel hurt and threatened. And many of them feel just plain insecure.

Men should be careful on this point. They should be sensitive to the feelings of their wives. I know men who are constantly guilty of mental torture. They seem to get a sadistic pleasure out of seeing their wives suffer because of their unending remarks about "this girl's legs" and "that woman's bust." They seem not to realize that the wife always takes this kind of statement as part one of an unfair comparison. Even if the husband does not say it, she feels, rightly or wrongly, that she is being compared. A woman knows that she cannot forever be a spring chicken and she would not like to be reminded of it, much less admit it.

Not long ago, I wrote a column entitled, "The ugly little wife." Just recently I received the following lovely letter from a troubled wife, which clearly illustrates my point.

Dear Bob,

Thank you for your writing the article on the ugly little wife! You are indeed God-sent, for it came at just the right time. I needed to be reminded that physical beauty is only secondary to spiritual beauty. I am one of those little wives. Maybe not "ugly" but it seemed so as my husband has been surrounded by acclaimed "beauties." I really felt very insecure, for it's quite difficult to compete with physical beauty. All the more difficult to recover my youth (if not impossible!) which is synonymous with the current standards of physical beauty. But your article made me think twice and realize that wives are more than just things to look at!

Thank you for writing a column in the newspaper. I am one of those who crave for spiritual readings that are down-to-earth. It's not really to flatter you, but I'm really grateful that you're around and you're the first one I read! I even clip your articles so I can re-read them.

I've been told that "your specialty" is about teenagers and their problems, but I don't think so. You're also tops on the subject of marriage. Please write often on your "specialty" for you are truly appreciated especially by one little ugly (?) wife.

Thank you.

Women are so fussy about beauty culture, not because of themselves or other women. They are finicky about their appearance because they know it means so much to their men. And because men place such a high premium on physical beauty, women are engaged in an unending battle to keep up with the latest beauty queen. Women know it is a losing fight. But they refuse to admit they are out of it until the day they die. They need to be reassured-even if it's not true-that they still have that sparkle in their eyes; that they have not lost their taste for attractive clothes; that they are still (pardon the expression) quite "sexy" in spite of their years.

In short, when it comes to physical beauty, most women enjoy living in a world of illusion where there are no runner-ups.

DATE WITH THE WIFE

THELMA IS A BEAUTIFUL woman. You would never think she is 35 years old and the mother of six. Though she is a busy housewife, Thelma always finds time to spend a while in the parlor getting herself all fixed up. So it isn't because she is not presentable that Rudy, her husband, never invites her out.

And when it comes to brains, Thelma has plenty. A college graduate and a scholar throughout school, this little woman is bright indeed. Even now, whenever she has a chance, she reads and tries to keep up with the times. So it isn't because she is dull that Rudy seems to be ashamed of her.

Personality? That is what Thelma has the most. She is the life of the party and feels at home with the high and the mighty, as well as the poorest of the poor.

Perhaps Thelma is so deeply hurt because she can find no logical reason for Rudy's apparent negligence in inviting her out to parties and business conferences. Oh, she knows that she would have to politely decline almost all his invitations because of the work in the house.

However, she would enjoy, on occasion, the thrill and the excitement of a dinner out.

Rudy, however, never seems to want her along. He keeps saying that a woman's place is in the home and that she would be bored anyway. But, behind all of his "reasons" and excuses," Thelma cannot help but feel that there is something more. In short, she has become convinced Rudy is somehow ashamed of her.

Of course, such is not the case. In fact, Rudy is very proud of his wife. There is no other woman in his life, either. It's just that he sincerely and deeply believes that his wife should stay at home with the kids. Rudy also feels that he would not want his wife to see the things he knows she will necessary witness at such gatherings. He also realizes that sometimes the meetings he attends get out of hand and he would not want the woman he loves to be embarrassed. So he keeps her at home.

I have heard countless wives complain to me that their husbands seem to be ashamed of them (many young ladies speak the same way about their boyfriends too!). Most of the time, beneath the griping, there is the strong suspicion that the husband is trying to hide something. Very often he is.

Many men keep their wives at home so that they can circulate more freely (often in and out of bedrooms) without the knowledge of the trusting wife. Countless "conferences" and "business meetings" have turned out to be occasions for movements towards the left. And many males would be hard put to give an account of some of their alleged "business" dinners. It really is not fair, but it happens all too often.

However, if a man is not fooling around, but sincerely believes that mom should stay at home or that she would be bored with some of his authentic business dinners, then he should at least make other arrangements to take his wife out for a meal once in a while.

When a woman begins to feel that her husband is no longer proud of her, she settles into a deep mood of bitterness and depression. She becomes bitter because she believes her husband cares more for others and gives more importance to those who are less deserving than her. A tragic proof of that is the great sadness that moves into her life.

No woman enjoys being put on the shelf and left there. Every wife longs to share her husband's life. She wants him to be proud of her and she sees these limited public appearances as opportunities for him to show her off to his friends.

When a man is sensitive to this need that his wife expresses, you can be sure that he will make her a happy woman indeed.

If you happen to be a married man or single and in love, take her out on the town as soon as the opportunity arises. Then sit back and enjoy her happy mood.

COMING HOME

THEY SAY THAT LIFE is made of thousands of multicolored tiny threads, all interwoven to form one meaningful tapestry. That love is a many-splendored thing composed of countless little things. In love, and especially in marital love, it is there that little things will make or break two people.

It is the daily bread of seemingly unimportant kindness that makes a marriage interesting and exciting. It is the many little thoughtful acts that add spice to married life. The momentous events (like the birth of a child, the marriage of a son) rarely occur in marriage. Rather, it is the little things, the common everyday happenings that will either thrill or bore a couple. It is for this reason that perhaps the greatest enemy of marriage is routine.

If a man is to remain successful not only in business but in the business of marriage, he must be very creative in devising ingenious methods that will cut into the routine of daily living.

If a wife is to keep her man and her family intact, she must know how to be consistently thrilling in the presence of her husband. All this is not easy. One must be alert in looking for opportunities to make a little thing something very meaningful and unforgettable.

Take, for instance, coming home. When a man leaves his work and heads for home, he should be eager to step into his house, not because it is a beautiful structure of wood and concrete but because of the lovely person who will be waiting to greet him upon his arrival. When a man comes home, he expects, rightly or wrongly, to be received as a special guest in his own home.

If he walks into the living room and finds his wife sprawled out on the sofa, he expects at least a slight sign of recognition. Sometimes all he gets is a sleepy nod of the head or a weak wave of the hand.

Some women do not realize what it means for a man to come home in the evening after a hard day's work. They don't know how much a man looks forward to entering the quiet sanctuary of his home. They rarely understand what a man expects when he comes home. Perhaps it is because few men speak about it except in moments of anger and frustration.

A woman can please a man immensely by noticing him when he comes home. The more she will please him. Little gestures like bringing him his slippers or offering him something to eat or fixing him a cold drink are all worth their weight in gold.

I have met countless men who, during the course of conversation concerning problems with their wives, have mentioned in passing the significance of this "coming home" ritual. You would be surprised, ladies, to learn how much importance men attach to it.

On the other hand, men much more than women, are insensitive to the part they play in the "coming home" ceremony. They expect to be served and waited upon hand and foot, but they hardly ever think of giving. When they walk into the house, they look for the red carpet and hope to hear the sound of trumpets. In other words, this is one occasion when they want to be treated as *head* of the family.

The husband must also understand the needs of his wife. He must remember that the boredom and the dreary routine of housekeeping have led her to expect more than a simple "Hi!" from her man when he walks through the door. Just as it costs very little in time, effort and money, for a woman to please her husband when he arrives home, so it is just as easy for the husband to make his wife happy when he first sees her after a whole day away from home.

How much does a candy bar, a card (even if it is not her birthday) cost? How much time does it take to write her a little note telling her that you miss her? Just three lines. How much extra energy is expended in a hug that is just a little bit stronger than the ordinary one or a kiss that lingers only a moment longer than the usual one?

Let's face it. We all too often neglect the little things that could make our lives so much richer. We pass up so many opportunities to make our relationships more vital and more dynamic. We dismiss with an "Oh … it's nothing," the chances to strengthen our love for one another.

If you are reading this in the office, you might think about it on your way home tonight. If you happen to be a housewife, you might still have time to bake his favorite dessert.

PEOPLE TALKING WITHOUT SPEAKING

ONE OF MY FAVORITE songs is "The Sound of Silence." Perhaps it is because of what I see and feel around me that its lyrics mean so much to me. I guess I could write countless commentaries about this beautiful piece of music.

However, there is just one line that is the subject of my thought today. Whenever I hear Simon and Garfunkel sing the words "people talking without speaking, people hearing without listening," I am reminded of the lines in one of the psalms in the bible which says: "They have eyes but they see not; they have ears but they hear not."

I am also reminded of many people whose courtships and marriages are spinning out of control. And of friends who are slowly but surely moving away from one another. In almost every case, they no longer really communicate with each other.

Oh yes! They talk about all kinds of things. But usually, they are things that do not really matter. They talk about trivialities and matters that are external to themselves. How many couples spend hours talking about nothing? How often have I seen people trying, all to no avail, to get past the "weather stage" of a conversation? And we have all known of couples who have not had an intimate and intense conversation in years.

And, horror of horrors, there are couples who no longer talk at all—not even about the weather. Some may go days and even weeks without even saying "hi." Think about what kind of a home that must be like. Hell should be a welcomed relief. And, by the way, can you imagine how the kids must feel growing up in a house (not a home), where the air is so tense and electric that the slightest spark could set off a tremendous explosion? And I wonder what thoughts must be racing through their minds when they witness a scene at the dinner table where one of the parents never speaks, nor looks up, whereas the other, trying to cover up and ease the tension, cannot keep quiet for three seconds?

The tragedy of such a scene is that one (or both parties) has given up the ship and admitted things are just about impossible. And what is worse, somebody has cut the communication lines that are essential if the already bad situation is to be rectified and properly corrected in time to avoid a disaster.

What worries me in such an instance is that one (or both partners) just doesn't seem to care anymore. And when there is indifference, there is no will to fight, no attempt to make an effort. And without this willingness, the situation stagnates and, in effect, deteriorates with the passing of each day. There is no spirit left, no drive. Nothing remains but a defeated, beaten individual.

How does one help such a couple? Without a doubt, the most important task is to reopen the lines of communications leading to the hearts of these troubled people.

Then, if it is possible to rekindle courtship's beautiful curiosity that has been lost, a newfound thirst for discovery and for understanding may come about. Then, and only then, is there a strong enough foundation upon which both partners may start rebuilding mutual love.

THE NEUTRAL CORNER

WHEN A FIGHTER SCORES a knockdown, he goes to a neutral corner and from there he watches his opponent try to struggle to his feet all by himself.

Life is full of neutral corners. There are plenty of them around and there is hardly one of us who does not at one time or another take refuge there from the many conflicts that face us.

How often do we refuse to get involved in a good cause? How many times do we turn our backs on people who are down on the canvas of life, trying desperately to get back on their feet? And when was the last time you turned your eyes away from a social injustice that was crying for a solution?

I think all of us make use of the neutral corner to excuse ourselves from involvement. We all, at one time or another, prefer to bury our heads in the sand and not know what is going on rather than assume the burdens of others.

Even in our relations with our friends, we often prefer to remain neutral rather than risk hurting someone we love. And there are times when our inactivity is the direct cause of the hurt.

In marriage, spouses are forever rushing into neutral corners. Take Jun, who is living with his parents. His wife Stella and his mother are continuously going at each other. Jun does not want to offend his wife whom he loves deeply by taking sides with his Mom. On the other hand, he loves and respects his mother and dares not go against her, even when she is clearly at fault.

As a result of his neutral stand, he irritates both his wife and his Mom. His wife, because she feels that he loves his mother more than her and refuses to see a reality that is obviously so glaring. His Mom, because she thinks her son is "ungrateful" and "disloyal" to the family.

Another more tragic case is that of the weak husband who abdicates his right as the head of the family and thus forces his wife to do all the dirty work of bringing up his kids.

When the children approach him to ask for permission to go to a party, he says, "ask you mother." When a problem arises in school, he tells his daughter, "see your mother." And when it comes to discipline, it is the poor woman who is made to feel like a tyrant. The father is so neutral that Mama has to do all the punishing and scolding while Dad buries his head in the newspaper or pretends to be asleep before the TV set. When you ask the kids what they think of Mom, they will tell you that she is "strict." "What about your father?" "Oh, he's okay, I guess ... he really doesn't say much."

Some people may be so weak that they just don't dare come out of the neutral corner ever. They are so weak and fragile that the slightest conflict (or even the simple thought of conflict) frightens them to death. They inevitably suffer from the paralysis of fear. They just cannot move.

There are, on the other hand, people who use the neutral corner as a deadly weapon to destroy others. They are the ones who get involved and involve others and push an unsuspecting person into a vulnerable position. And when the going gets rough, they back out and rush into the nearest neutral corner and leave their trusting victim all by himself.

Neutrality is fine when what is going on around you is none of your business. It is desirable when it can be used to mediate differences of opinion. It is at its greatest when it serves to bring people together. But when used as an escape from reality and responsibility, it is pure and unadulterated cowardice.

HOW TO FIGHT YOUR MAN

VICTOR IS BY NATURE a fiery person. He is quick-tempered and when he explodes, he says a lot of things he inevitably regrets after he has cooled off. Victor is married and, to be very honest, he has not been exactly an ideal husband.

During his 16 years of married life, he has made a few "left turns." Luckily, his wife Norma and his five kids know nothing of these short-lived affairs. However, there are other faults that he has that are glaring—even to his children. And if his teenagers can even notice some of his personality flaws, Norma is still the most knowledgeable of all.

It often happens that they have some very violent arguments. And since Norma is no cool kitten either, it sometimes gets to be terribly noisy in their bedroom. A few times, Victor has even raised his hand against his wife.

Norma loves Victor deeply. She does not enjoy arguing with her husband. However, her character is such that she cannot seem to allow anything that gets on her nerves to pass without making a pointed remark. All too often, her words are offensive and nasty. Victor, of course, gets hurt and fights right back and then the battle is on.

When two volatile characters like Norma and Victor live together, you can expect explosions and fire and, when things really get out of hand, ashes.

The difficulty with such a relationship is that both are so high-strung and quick on the trigger that outbursts occur often and unexpectedly. And, instead of ending just as quickly, they are prolonged because both parties just refuse to call off the argument.

Conflicts and tensions in marriage are as inevitable as the sunset. Married couples that expect to live their lives in total and complete relaxation, free from any and all difficulties, have read too many romance novels. Of course, there will be trouble. You can be one hundred and three percent sure of it.

However, most married people (and sweethearts too) do not know how to handle explosive partners. Instead of calming their loved ones, they unknowingly make matters worse. You don't put out a fire by dousing it with gasoline. In fact, when a conflagration gets out of control, all attempts must be made to contain it. And sometimes the most effective method is to let it burn itself out.

When a woman has on her hand a hot-tempered man who wants to fight, the best way to argue with him is not to. Trying to explain matters to an angry man is like attempting to converse with a person in an automobile that is spinning out of control.

If you want to get a message across to somebody, don't even try when he is emotionally upset. He just is not in any position to listen. Sure, he will hear your words, but they will not mean a thing. He will be like the people in the song "Sound of Silence," which says, "People talking without speaking; people hearing without listening."

For soothing, calming effects, try SWAS (silence with a smile). SWAS will usually disarm even the most noisy character, especially if he loves you. No real man enjoys fighting with a smiling wall. It makes him feel cheap to be blasting away at a cute little smiling creature who is just standing there with a pretty and wide grin.

Later, when the stormy seas have subsided, you can talk sense. And nobody gets hurt either. And the guy feels worse than ever for having shouted at his little woman, who did not even fight back.

So the next time your man flares up and challenges you to draw your gun, don't. Instead, pull out your smile and blast him in the heart.

HOW TO HOLD A HUSBAND

How do you hold a husband?

How does a girl keep her sweetheart?

Interesting questions for those not in love. Vital questions for people in love, whether this love be deep or shallow.

Just recently I heard a very beautiful story about a teenaged wife who was walking along the beach one day with her Mom. She asked her mother: "How does a woman hold her husband?"

The Mama knew her daughter was expecting a long speech and hours of advice. Instead, the older woman stopped and picked up two handfuls of sand. She held the sand in her right hand tightly and squeezed hard. The sand fell through her fingers. The tighter she squeezed, the more sand fell to the ground.

The other hand, she kept open. The sand stayed. The daughter immediately understood what her mother was trying to tell her.

The tighter the restrictions a woman places on her husband, the more the chances of losing him. The more possessive a woman is, the more apt she is to end up with nothing.

No man likes to be policed. The male holds to his freedom more dearly than does the female whose very nature it is to be more dependent. A man appreciates a woman who trusts him. In fact, this confidence is so very important that I cannot see how any relationship can last without it. Sooner or later you can expect the man to get fed up and break his chains and flee.

It is also true that countless men abuse the trust their wives show them. In fact, many males hide behind the "trust mask" in order to play Don Juan. I have met men who feign indignation when their wives suspect them of unfaithfulness. But in reality, they are using this technique to lay down a smoke screen to hide their left turns. In other words, their appeal for trust is only a diversionary tactic, which is meaningless because it is insincere.

This question of trust has to be a two-way street. "Sure I trust you," says the intelligent wife, "but I expect you not to double-cross me either. And should you abuse the confidence I have put in you, don't expect me to continue trusting you blindly forever."

The truth of the matter is that when a woman has been deceived, it is extremely difficult for her to trust a man completely again. Chances are that there will always be some reservations in the back of her mind. And you cannot really blame her either. When you place all your chips in trust with the man you love and admire most and then later discover that he has been stealing from you, anybody can understand why you would hesitate to continue giving him money for safekeeping.

I suppose what is most important is that, from the very beginning, costly mistakes should be avoided. When two people are honest with each other, they do not really give each other reason to doubt. However, if a man and a woman begin to be dishonest in little things, suspicions about the more important things in life are expected. Rarely is the consistently honest couple in deep marital trouble.

THE FIRST MOVE

THINGS HAVE NOT BEEN going very well between Teddy and Celia. Frequent quarrels and conflicts have created tension, which has become oppressive.

Both husband and wife seem to dislike being separated by the wall of uncomfortable silence which has arisen between them, however, neither one of them seems able to do anything about it. Both are frozen in very awkward positions.

Teddy knows that he should perhaps say something. Celia is convinced that just one little act, one gesture, could break the ice and get both of them talking again.

However, the big problem seems to be that neither wants or is capable of making the first move.

It is a tragedy when a love relationship is struck by this terrible paralysis. Both parties want to act, but neither knows just how. Husband and wife have become like two little teenagers who had a fight and don't know how to make up.

The first move is always the hardest. When in conflict and tension, all the parties concerned are afraid and feel threatened. And when people are threatened, they become defensive. Defensive people, in turn, are very suspicious and wary of others.

Unless Teddy and Celia break the deadlock, things will continue to deteriorate. The silence and the distance created will provoke more misunderstanding and conflicts. And since what is needed to eliminate the tension is communication, somebody had better make the first move and start talking.

Most people believe that pride is what prevents a person from making the first move. I think that it is fear more than anything else. Fear of being embarrassed if rejected. Fear of making matters worse by saying the wrong word. Fear of fouling up the situation with a poor sense of timing.

What I mean to say is that most people want reconciliation. Nobody enjoys that uncomfortable feeling of having an enemy. Nobody thrives on a misunderstanding. In such a situation, everybody stands to lose.

Whenever two people are in conflict and unable or afraid to make the first move, my job as a counselor is quite simple. I have to convince one of the parties to risk making a sincere first move.

If the move is loaded with sincerity, you can be sure that there will be a very favorable response from the other party who senses this and also wants the whole unpleasant situation to end.

Many people (especially teenagers) believe that making the first move will be interpreted as a sign of weakness by the other party. It probably will be if the person is immature and childish.

However, if there is maturity and any degree of perception present, you can be sure that a sincere first move will be interpreted as a sign of care and affection. It will be seen in effect, as an act of love and a serious attempt at reconciliation without the risk of personal rejection.

If you who are reading these lines remember that you and a friend have been stalemated and have been living in cold silence for quite some time, I would suggest that you start thinking of making the first move.

TRAPPED BY IN-LAWS

RUDY, NINETEEN YEARS OLD, and Minda, eighteen, are separated after less than a year of marriage. They still love one another deeply. However, conditions in the house of her in-laws became so intolerable that Minda left in a huff and returned to her mother's home.

Rudy called me and asked me to help get his wife back. I said I would try. We made an appointment and, thirty minutes ahead of schedule. I found them sitting close together outside my office. They seemed very happy and were holding hands and mushing it up a little bit. They looked more like sweet teenagers than separated people.

After talking a while, it was obvious to me that sending Minda back to the house of her in-laws was out of the question. She had been hurt too deeply. The husband's family exhibited deep seated hostile feelings and maintained a firm and unforgiving stance.

The marriage would never work in that house. Clearly, Rudy and Minda would have to find an apartment outside (the farther from the in-laws, the better) if they were to have a second chance. And with Minda eight months pregnant, a second chance was definitely in order.

I talked with the husband's mom. She definitely wore the pants in the family. No question about that. She was a hard woman who did not hesitate to show her contempt for her daughter-in-law. She emphatically stated, in no uncertain terms, that she didn't care if she never saw the girl again. And it was obvious to all that she hoped to discourage any attempt at reconciliation.

That's when I began to do some talking. I reminded her that her attitude was perhaps the most formidable obstacle to her son's happiness. I also told her that she had no right to decide for her son. She replied that she wasn't deciding anything, but that she was merely expressing her opinion on the matter. I answered that she was, in effect, using economic blackmail to make her opinion a reality. "You know," I told her, "that your son is financially incapable of supporting his wife. Likewise, you are also aware that the girl cannot return to your house under the present circumstances. And, you will make it hard on your son if he tries to live with his wife's family. Besides, they are so angry at him that to send him there would just reverse the roles. He would be the persecuted one. Obviously, the answer lies in getting an apartment away from both families and giving them a place where they can recover and allow the deep wounds to heal. If you do not help him financially, then this will be next to impossible."

It was a tough job. But after a couple of stormy hours, the mother finally gave in and agreed to pay for the rent of a small apartment. Today, Rudy and Minda (and little Carlos) are together again. Relations with the in-laws are still not ideal but improving. And it looks like the young couple will make it.

The names above have been changed and the circumstances modified, but the story is basically one that I have heard repeated often during my counseling sessions. Since most often a mother (not to speak of the rest of the family) is expected to side with her own child, the other party is at a distinct disadvantage. And the moment the in-laws get mixed up in the internal affairs of marriage, they are almost sure to mess things up. They are too close and too emotionally involved to render an unbiased judgment.

Furthermore, the young couple living with in-laws does not feel comfortable. Every disagreement, every quarrel is known to the whole household. They live in a glass cage and cannot usually work out their own problems without unsolicited outside interference. Privacy is important to newlyweds. They rarely get it living with in-laws.

It is also of great importance that a young housewife has her own little domain; that she be allowed to run her own house and gain self-confidence. You cannot expect the mother-in-law, who has reigned supreme in her home for thirty years to step down. So the young wife remains a permanent guest in a household that she very often considers hostile.

If perhaps you happen to be a reader who is living with his or her in-laws, please start planning to move out and set up your own house-even if things are going well. Time can bring about many changes.

And if you happen to be a mother-in-law with young married people in your house, then, for your own sake and theirs, try and help them to get out and set up their own home as soon as possible.

Parents very often attempt to keep their children close to them even after they get married. Nothing wrong with that. Sometimes, though, they insist on having them in the same house. They often find, to their utter dismay, that this only serves to tear into little pieces a relationship that was formerly very beautiful. You can be close without being in the same house.

BIOLOGY POWER

"**BOB, I JUST COULDN'T** help it."
"I don't understand myself."
"Bob, it happened so quickly."
"I guess we forgot ourselves."

All these quotes are real and not imagined. They were uttered by men and women who got themselves into big trouble because they did not understand that unbelievably mysterious and mighty reality I like to call BIOLOGY POWER.

Every normal man and woman has a biological make-up that is subject to certain laws. These laws govern us strictly and any fooling around with them usually means trouble.

A woman is in possession of a reproductive system that dominates her whole being. She was created to bear children and her physical make-up has such a powerful explosive potential that it takes less than most women suspect to trigger off a violent reaction. Subdued lighting, a touch of the hand, the right word, all are potential fuses that could cause a woman's biology power to burst into action. Then anything can happen. And usually, it's trouble.

I used to think that women could control their sexual drive and suppress it whenever they liked. After talking to countless women who got into all kinds of trouble, I now believe that there can come a moment between a man and a woman when control and judgment are just about impossible. Just as a car moving down a highway can accelerate from 20 kph to 80 kph almost unnoticeably, so can a friendship give a rise to blinding passion in no time.

Everybody, of course, is aware of the hair-trigger sexual mechanism that lies within the male. That it takes very little to put the biology power of the male to work, is known to all. That is almost every day. There are some women who, to their tragic disadvantage, have had to learn the hard way. There are other females who have studied the weaknesses of men and have used their knowledge to exploit and to destroy.

Men and women who want to throw themselves headlong into uncontrolled sexual activities should find no difficulty at all in doing so. It is those who are mindful of their responsibilities and want to use their sexual powers in a mature way who have to be on the alert so as not to fall into the many unsuspecting traps.

I suppose the best defense lies in the security of knowing that one is weak and that anything can and will happen unless utmost caution and vigilance are exercised at all times.

A woman should convince herself that there is a limit to her ability to say "no"; that she has a point of no return; that things can happen with lightning speed.

The man, on the other hand, should never forget that God created him with such an aggressive sexual drive that just about every woman is a potential bed partner—whether he loves her or not. He should understand that his biology does not distinguish between the loved one and the "other girl" who just happens to come onto the scene.

These things should especially be explained to the young people who are not experienced in life. And those responsible for this education are the parents. Should Mom and Dad feel they are unable or unwilling to do so, they are duty-bound to find somebody who can and will.

A HOUSE IS NOT A HOME

"**A CHAIR IS STILL** a chair
Even when there's no
one sitting there.
But a chair is not a house
And a house is not a home
When there's no one
there to hold you tight.
No one there to kiss
you goodnight."

The above lines are taken from a song that was popular some time ago. It is a painfully beautiful song. Beautiful in its sensitive awareness of the deep sufferings found in the unhappy family. The author of these lines must have surely felt the almost unbearable loneliness that comes with the realization that love is no more.

These are many beautiful houses that are far from being homes. In fact, there are some fabulous mansions that are luxurious hells. Husbands often delude themselves into thinking that as long as they provide a house and lot and all the other trimmings of the good life, they've performed their duties as the head of the family.

Most people believe that if a man is a "good provider," he is the model family man. "Providing" is almost always at the top of the list of priorities in marriage. I agree.

However, what many people fail to see, is that "providing" means more than building a new house, sending the kids to the best schools and bringing home a fat paycheck. It also means "providing" enough TLC (Tender Loving Care) to create a healthy environment in which the whole family can grow in maturity and mutual love. Some well-meaning husbands spend plenty of money on their children. However, when the teenager asks Dad to attend the school play in which she has a bit part, he is "too busy providing."

Doctors of the mind tell us that many men who feel inadequate as fathers try to compensate for their lack of deep love and warmth by "providing" their families with more than enough material benefits.

I have heard countless disappointed teenagers say: "Bob, my dad gives me everything I want and need—except love." Or, "I don't care for all these things Bob. What I want is for us to be happy." How tragic! How horribly frustrating for the head of the family to discover that he is a failure in spite of his sincere hard work.

Young people—and the wife too—long for a happy home. Boarding houses are common. The security that a warm home affords is harder to come by. It is a sad fact that so many dissatisfied adolescents see their fathers as playing the role of the hotel manager. The teenager comes home from school to a house that has its rules and regulations. He takes his merienda, goes to "his room" for a while, then decides to step out. He returns late at night after his parents have retired. The next morning, he is off again without seeing either Mom or Dad. To so many youngsters like him, home is more accurately referred to as "home base."

To become a father is quite easy. But to head a family correctly is an awesome 24-hour job. It means an effective division of time between offices. It means sacrificing some of the fun a man is genuinely entitled to in order to just be home with the family. It means getting to know one's sons and daughters at least as well as one's job. The man who is a father not only in name but in fact, understands that "bringing up the children" is as much his work of love and is not to be surrendered unconditionally to his wife.

If a father feels that his children (and his wife) are moving away from him; if he feels that he is a stranger in his own house, he should do something quickly to stop matters from deteriorating further. He should tackle his job of getting back "on the inside" seriously as he would handle a major problem that is a threat to his job. Otherwise, he may find himself maintaining and financing some teenagers (his kids) who look upon him as a convenient bank account and who run to other "close friends" for advice and consolation. He should realize that if he is too busy for his family, then he is just too busy. Period.

THE NAGGER

IF YOU HAPPEN TO BE a woman and you want to drive your husband or your boyfriend crazy, try nagging. This is just about the best way I know to push a man to his wit's end. There is also no better way to turn off a husband or lose a sweetheart.

Surely, nagging is one of the most common complaints I hear from disenchanted husbands. A woman can be a terrible cook and a man can bear it. She can have bad breath, a cranky mother-in-law, and ugly legs. He can take it. But, if she is one of these intolerable creatures people refer to as "naggers," then she is just too much for most men.

The nagger is hardly ever found in a happy family. She thrives, though, in a discontented home.

"You're always drunk," she screams. She is right. He does come home drunk most of the time.

"You're seeing that woman again," she says sarcastically. Right again. He just came from her apartment. "You're forever coming home late," she shouts in frustration. Again she is right. He hates to come to the house when she is still awake because he knows he will be greeted with the old familiar lines once again.

"You're no good," she says finally. Right again! And after hearing it so often, he believes it.

The tragedy of this nagging business is that the nagger is usually right. That's what makes her so despicable—she's always right. She keeps repeating day in and day out the facts of the case. And the shameful truth keeps ringing in the guilty man's ears. He is continually reminded of things he would rather forget.

He cannot reply, because he really has no solid defense. So he imitates the marines under fire. He digs a hole and dives in and silently waits for the artillery barrage to end. Or he may refuse to listen and proceed to shout her down. Or, he might stalk out of the house and join his friends in order to try and forget her unpleasantness.

The woman, on the other hand, feels thoroughly frustrated. He just cannot seem to "understand." Or he refuses to change. In any case, it all seems hopeless because, in spite of her constant reminders, nothing happens.

"But Bob," you may ask, "what should I do?" Try something else. What exactly? I don't really know. It depends on the situation. Try anything, but please don't nag. You can only make matter worse. Your husband is intelligent. He is aware of the problem. Even though you do not remind him daily, he cannot forget. The trick is to help him to do what he is convinced he must do.

Nagging has hardly ever brought about the desired change. It has, though, most often embittered men and driven a wedge between them and their wives.

TEMPTATION OF A MARRIED MAN

HE WASN'T UNHAPPY ... Not really. It was just that things were not nearly as exciting as they used to be when he was courting his beautiful wife. It wasn't that Norma had lost any of the beauty that had captivated him when he first saw her. In fact, if anything, found her more beautiful than ever. Perhaps it was because at 33, she had learned to carry herself with the dignity and poise that are signs of a mature woman.

Maybe, at 35, Nanding was bored. Twelve years of relative happiness in marriage, four beautiful and intelligent children, and a secure executive position in a prosperous company. What more could a man ask for? Nevertheless, Nanding felt that life was passing him by. Perhaps, he had been too successful. There didn't seem to be many challenges left around for him to tackle. Up until just then, he had little time for anything other than his work and his growing family.

Now, all of a sudden he had the desire to fool around with women. Not that he had never felt like making left turns before. There were always plenty of temptations (and on occasion a little bit of wandering) but nothing as serious as this. For the first time in his married life, he had been entertaining the thought of carrying on a full-blown affair. And what confused him most, was the fact that now he often caught himself making plans in the deep recesses of his mind.

Could it be that he was really falling in love with Myrna, that 22-year old accountant who worked just across the hall? Or was it just infatuation? She certainly had the potential of a beauty queen.

Perhaps what unnerved him most was the way the girl seemed to respond to his teasing and half-serious remarks. Unless he was terribly mistaken, Myrna was beginning to fall head over heels for him. And he thought that quite flattering.

Despite his receding hairline and expanding waistline, it was very refreshing to know that a beautiful young lady like Myrna could bypass the hordes of eligible wolves who continuously stalked her, and turn all her attention to a man 13 years her senior, married and the father of four.

Soon Nanding and Myrna were lunching together quite regularly. She found him mature, soft-spoken, and very affectionate (unlike the boisterous twenty-year-olds around her who couldn't keep an intelligent conversation going for ten minutes and who only thought of going to bed). Not that Myrna didn't arouse him sexually. She did. But he was able to camouflage his feelings well (married men are usually pretty good at that).

Myrna felt sure Nanding loved her deeply. At first, the fact that he had a wife and kids troubled her quite a bit, but she justified herself by reasoning that "it's okay if you're really in love with each other." But she was wrong. Nanding didn't "really" love her. I guess he was very fond of her. But deep love? No. He surely loved his wife more deeply. However, he found Myrna exciting. She was always pretty (he never saw her getting up in the morning) and fresh-looking, forever attentive to his every need.

Norma, on the other hand, continuously complained of being tired. He felt bored with the same old conversations about the house, the kids, and the relatives. None of that with Myrna, who didn't have that "cooped-up-housewife" attitude. With her, no boring talk of the house. No problems with report cards, discipline, and homework. A feeling, the like of which he had not felt since the days of his courtship, swept him along and, eventually, into the arms of his newfound mistress.

Then, one evening, the expected happened. Nanding and Myrna committed adultery. Now, more than ever, the young girl clung to her lover. It happened again and again until, one fine day, Norma caught them.

Nanding confessed everything to his wife, who threatened to separate unless he walked away from his mistress immediately and forever.

To make a long story short, after a lot of heartaches and embarrassing moments (not to mention the bits of scandal that got out) Nanding left Myrna and went back to his wife. Things were never the same again, though.

I did not write this to entertain. I meant it to be a simple reminder to married women that the competition for your husband did not end with your touching walk to the altar. Remember that getting a husband is easy enough. Holding him for a lifetime is something else again!

There are countless married men whose stories are similar to Nanding's. Just about every husband encounters such temptations. Of this, every wife must be constantly aware. I said *aware*, not *jealous*.

Guard your marriage. Keep yourself pretty for your husband. Try to find out if you are boring him. Think up interesting things to talk about (like you used to do when you were being courted). Love him dearly. Make him feel important and indispensable (even if he's not). Remember, there are plenty of women (married and single) who would go to great lengths to get their itchy hands on your husband. To keep him, you've got to compete with them. Sometimes you've got to fight for him.

WHEN IT HURTS TO TELL THE TRUTH

The voice on the telephone was unmistakably that of a worried teenager. “Bob, I’ve got a problem.” “Yes, what is it? Can I help?” “Bob, I have a boyfriend. We have been going together for many months now. When he first visited me he wanted to meet my parent. He liked my Mom very much. I told him my Dad is dead and he said, I’m sorry about that. But yesterday he learned that I lied to him … he was so angry. My Dad is not dead. He’s very much alive. The truth is that he separated from my mother many years ago. What am I going to do?”

Unusual? No. this frightened, confused little lady is only one of the countless millions who daily get themselves into all sorts of trouble because of a basic lack of honesty.

Whether it be a scared teenager lying about her family background or an employee padding an expense account or a husband fooling his unsuspecting wife, every day, people are weaving a sinister web of lies in order to cover up their deceptions. What they fail to realize is that like the carefree fly buzzing around in the piggery, that spider web of lies will eventually be their death trap.

In my daily counseling of countless people with all sorts of problems, I have found that one of the ever-present causes of the difficulties encountered is some sort of dishonesty. People just do not seem to be brave enough to tell the truth and face the music if need be. They prefer to take the easy way out and lie or tell a half-truth.

Most of the misunderstandings, if you will notice, are caused by dishonest acts, and/or words that are deceptive. An irate husband shouts at his wife for being flirt at the party they just attended. Actually, she feels that he has not been giving her the attention she deserves so she decided to make him just a little bit jealous by spending a lot of time with a handsome bachelor. By turning on the charm full blast, she really caused her husband to boil inside. And it took all his self-control not to make a scene during the gathering. The wife, now faced with her furious husband, makes matters worse by adding fuel to the fire: "I think he's such a nice guy" (actually she thinks he's a bore).

Her husband slaps her and she weeps. She now begins to explain that it was just a game she was playing; that she doesn't really care for the guy; that she only intended to create a little jealousy.

By this time, his wife has acted out her part so convincingly that her husband no longer believes her. What started out as a game has ended in a monumental conflict that has left two people deeply hurt, a marriage with another deep wound and a substantial loss of trust and confidence on the part of the husband. All this because of a lack of honest behavior.

Sincerity is becoming a neglected virtue. Everyone admits that people "are but human" and that "everybody makes mistakes." However, few of us like to join the human race. It's okay in theory, but it hurts to be "human" because that means telling the whole world of our limitations and weaknesses.

How many guys make themselves out to be what they are not while courting a woman? The play works for a while. But you cannot act forever. Sooner or later, what you really are will see through the surface. Then, the game is over and all is lost.

I remember a young girl who had a phone pal. For weeks she spent long hours on the telephone conversing with the guy. She soon developed deep feelings of love for him. But she feared he would never reciprocate because she was confined to a wheelchair. So, in desperation, she hid the truth from him by fabricating all kinds of stories about herself that were pure fantasy.

The young man, completely taken in by her tactic, began to love her (or what he thought was her). He insisted on seeing her personally and meeting her family. She had to put him off for fear she would be discovered. The game went on for weeks until, in understandable frustration, the guy gave her the alternative: "See me or let's finish everything."

She was now with her back to the wall. It was either not tell him and surely lose him or tell him and take her chances. She told him. He was so overwhelmed that at first he did not want to believe his ears. How could she have lied to him for so long? His confidence and trust shattered (could he ever believe her again?), he left her without a word.

Had the girl told him the truth from the very beginning, I think she would have stood a much better chance of holding him.

Being sincere and telling the whole truth sometimes hurts. But it has its distinct advantages. For one thing, there is hardly any credibility gap. People will believe you more quickly. And should you readily admit to a mistake, most will be sympathetic and will find it easy to dismiss your slip.

On the other hand, lies and deception only postpone the inevitable appearance of the truth. They also cause anxiety and insecurity, for one never knows when somebody will stumble onto the truth. They also cause needless and unnecessary worry as to how one will explain away his lie and half-truths when caught.

I believe one of the surest ways to a peaceful and serene life is to get into the habit of telling the truth and dealing honestly with people.

SHOULD SHE OR SHOULDN'T SHE

LILY IS A VERY CHARMING and exceedingly beautiful girl. Though she is only 23-years old, she has had many suitors. And now, after an exciting courtship with Neny, she is busy preparing for her wedding day, which is fast approaching.

But, despite her seemingly happy disposition, Lily remains a very troubled girl. Unknown to her fiancé and friends, a fearful burden lies heavy on her troubled heart. She cannot discuss it with her friends and dares not to tell the man who has so completely won her loyalty and who means everything to her. Her problem is so deeply personal that she cannot confide it to anyone. What is it that troubles Lily? Why this tremendous fear? What can she not reveal to the man who is to be her husband?

Lily's problem started four years ago when Victor was her steady. At the time, both were so serious with one another, that Lily felt certain Victor would soon ask for her hand in marriage. Then one evening, after a movie, it happened.

The session of passionate kissing they experienced on the balcony served to excite both of them so much, that before Lily went home that night, she had lost her virginity. She felt bad about it but took comfort in the consoling promise of marriage Victor kept repeating to her.

However, things did not work out as planned. Four months later, after a number of visits to motels, her boyfriend suddenly lost interest in her. He no longer visited as often. They quarreled repeatedly and he seemed bored in her presence. Then one day, she discovered another girl in Victor's life. Soon, after a confrontation, he left her.

It took a while for Lily to recover. At first, she did not care to entertain males. She kept pretty much to herself. Eventually, though, time healed the gaping wound inflicted by Victor, and Lily began partying again. Then she met Benny, the wonderful man whose love and kindness made her alive again.

And now, everything she had hoped for—a whirlwind courtship, a loving man, a marriage proposal—all this had become a reality. But what if she told Benny about her past? Would it make a difference? Would he still love her, or would everything collapse? Should she wait until after marriage to tell him and take a chance on his love and understanding? But would Benny really understand?

Lily's predicament is not uncommon. Many troubled women share her problem and her perplexity. Should she tell or shouldn't she? I know that people—especially men—have strong feelings and convictions about this question.

I believe that a woman should confess her past affair to her fiancé and not wait until after the wedding to tell him. Otherwise, he may feel cheated and deceived. And when a man begins to think that his new wife has not been honest in this matter of sex, then he starts suspecting all sorts of things, and before you know it, the marriage is spinning out of control.

I know of some factual cases of a young husband who actually separated upon learning about the premarital sexual experiences of the new bride with another man. At any rate, I think the risk is too great to take. I did not always believe this way. However, experience with couples who have encountered this problem has caused my convictions to evolve. I go along with honesty as the best policy.

Anyway, if a man really loves a woman intensely, he can forgive a past mistake committed before they even met. If he leaves her because of this, then I don't think he loves her an awful lot.

Furthermore, I always advise a woman not to tell her fiancé until he is just about to set a definite date for the wedding. "Next year," is not specific enough. I know of some women who waited patiently for three, four, or five years for "next year" to materialize. And often, "next year" never comes.

The reasons for waiting until the last minute before the formal wedding announcement are two-fold. First, if the guy does not yet love a woman enough to want to marry her, what happened in the past remains so deeply personal that it's none of his business. Besides, if she tells him after the first few dates, chances are that he may either walk away or try to take advantage of her because he thinks she is an "easy touch." Once he loves her enough to propose marriage, the girl stands a better chance of holding him. At least it's not easy to walk off.

A brief word to men who are willing to accept a woman "despite her past." If you are going to accept her, then accept her completely. Don't talk about her past after your marriage—especially during an argument. If you are not willing and *able* to forget, then I suggest you gently step aside and let a more understanding man marry her.

Most of all, if young women were not so naive and could only cultivate a more realistic approach to love and sex; if they thought more often about the possible consequences of not waiting till marriage, then, there would be no need for this chapter.

THE BREAKING POINT

A WHILE BACK, THE SONG entitled "By the Time I Get to Phoenix," became very popular. As it often happens, most people sang bits and pieces of the lyrics without understanding the message the author was trying to convey.

The song, in effect, tells of a tired husband who, after countless arguments and conflicts, has reached the saturation point in his relationship with his wife. Thoroughly fed up and unable to bear the tension any longer, he leaves her, never to return.

The moral of this song is no stranger to me. Almost daily, I interview men and women who have reached the breaking point in their marriage. After months, sometimes years, of mounting pressure, the lid blows off and everything spills out.

There is nobody who does not have a breaking point. You can bend a branch just so much before it snaps. Likewise, every man, woman and child, have a set limit to the tension he/she can absorb.

Marriage is often very much like a volcano. Problems simmer beneath the surface. There are rumblings in the form of unresolved conflicts that weigh heavily on the heart of the troubled spouse. And unless there is some kind of action taken to relieve the tension, you can expect the pressure to become so unbearable that an eruption into open conflict is inevitable.

A woman must be a keen observer of her husband. She must remain always aware of the sensitivities of the man she loves and professes to understand so well. It is ironic that the wives who boast most about how thoroughly they "know" their husband are usually the ones who get the surprise of their life when the guy walks out.

I remember a woman sobbing uncontrollably while telling me about her husband's affair with a pretty hostess. She couldn't understand why he would set the girl up in an apartment and visit her daily. After talking with the man. I got the picture. He told me that his wife was such an unbearable nagger that coming home to her was a veritable torture. He was the silent type who hardly ever raised his voice. However, on a number of occasions he had begged his wife to give him peace. She did not see the warning signals, or if she did, paid no attention to them.

Some women—and men also—miscalculate the ability of their spouses to take emotional punishment. The woman who continuously dares her husband to leave the house may be the last to believe he would really do such a thing. Actually, had she been more sensitive to his hurt feelings, she would have noticed him inching his way towards the door weeks and months before.

The husband who callously ignores his unhappy wife's pleas and continues to openly display his mistress should not be surprised if one day he comes home and finds an empty house.

The vital question is: how far can I go before my husband explodes? How much can my wife take before she gets fed up?

A person cannot bear tension forever. It is unbelievable how much one can withstand, but nobody can hold out indefinitely. Like an infected boil that gives rise to painful swelling in the same way, long-standing conflicts must be resolved or at least worked on if the marriage is to be saved from fatal contagion.

SHOTGUN MARRIAGE

DELIA COULD NOT BELIEVE IT. The doctor had to be mistaken. It just couldn't be true. Yet it was. She was six weeks pregnant.

The 20-year-old felt growing panic in her heart. Nobody knew about it yet. But how long could she hide her secret? She had visions of grinning people staring at her big belly.

And what would her parents say? And her friends? What would they think when she would drop out of school in the middle of the next semester?

Her thoughts turned to Al, her 23-year-old sweetheart, who was still unaware of her condition. What would he say? Would he suggest marriage? She believed he would. After all, they had made plans often during their two-year courtship. And when he talked to her into bed, he had assured her that if anything happened, he would marry her. She remembered how those words broke down the last remaining barriers.

They had sexual intercourse a number of times. At first, Delia felt uncomfortable. The motel seemed hardly the place to express the deep love she felt in her heart for

Al. Yet he insisted that it was the only safe place. She didn't like the idea of sneaking in and out of these establishments of ill repute. She felt a tremendous amount of tension and fear of being discovered, but her love for this man overcame her anxieties and she was willing to take her chances.

Now, as she dialed Al's number, she felt consoled. He would surely understand. He loved her so. When Al's Mom called him to the phone, Delia felt so relieved.

"Al, I've got something very important to tell you, she said.

"What is it, Delia?"

"Al … I'm six weeks pregnant."

"What?"

"It's true … I just saw the doctor today."

"Oh, no!"

"Al … what are we going to do?"

"I don't know.'

Later, Al and Delia met to discuss their problem. Al suggested having an abortion. He said he would handle the expenses. Delia cried. She told him that she just couldn't kill the baby. "Besides," she wept, "it's ours. Al, how can you think of such a thing?"

"But, Delia … we have no choice. I can't marry you now … I'm not yet ready."

And so, the discussion went on late into the night. When Al took her home, her heart sank with the realization that Al didn't really intend to marry her. It was obvious—even to a girl blindly in love—that he was searching for all kinds of excuses not to settle down with her. Of course, he had a few good reasons also. He was graduating in few months and was jobless. Needless to say, he had no savings and would have to be completely dependent on his or her parents for their livelihood.

The following day, Delia told her mother. At first, her Mom refused to believe it. Then, when reality hit home with full force, she wept. Within hours, the household was in turmoil. Delia's father was violently angry. He kicked the furniture and shouted at his confused daughter.

The aunties and uncles were called in and a compadre who was an attorney was consulted.

Then from the angry lips of Delia's father came the solemn statement everyone had been expecting: "You must get married."

During the ensuing visits to Al's home, it was evident that the young man still did not *really* want to marry Delia. However, after listening to the girl's parents lecture him on his "responsibility" and their daughter's honor and the family's good name, Al reluctantly agreed to the marriage.

The situation that Al and Delia got themselves into is not rare. In fact, it happens more often than most people care to admit.

Whenever young people and their parents come to me with this problem, I immediately put all kinds of obstacles in the way of a wedding. I don't like "shotgun" weddings. Some of them work out. However, it has been my experience that the overwhelming majority of them are unhappy and all too many simply collapse a short while later.

When an unwed girl gets pregnant, she usually panics. She craves security and is more than willing to jump to any kind of safety—even if it is only temporary. She rarely thinks of all the consequences married life entails. And the decision to marry is so serious and sweeping that it should not be taken by a scared and confused little girl. The choice of a lifelong partner is tough enough, even in the best of conditions. Parents should not force a hasty decision on their children regardless of the smear on the family name. Besides, what about that name when their daughter ends up a separated woman and with three kids at the age of 26? What then? What happens when, out of loneliness and desperation, she becomes the reluctant mistress of a married man?

But what about the baby? You don't get married because of the baby. I am thinking about the child and the unhappy home in which he is destined to be reared. A house is not a home when there's no love there.

But what should be done if they don't get married? There are a number of other solutions which, for lack of space here, will have to be the subject of another chapter.

But of one thing I am certain. One error does not justify another. If two young people make the mistake of going to bed together, they and their child should not have to pay for it with a lifetime of misery.

ABSENCE MAKES THE HEART GROW COLDER

Doris and Sonny are very sad lovers indeed. Both are 24 years old and have been going steady for two years now. Next month, Sonny is scheduled to leave for the States, where he will pursue his medical career for three years.

Doris finds it difficult to smile because her heart is heavy with the knowledge that it is impossible for her to follow. Three years is a long time. When you're deeply in love, three years is almost forever.

Now, they are asking me what I think of their plans to get married just before Sonny's departure. My answer comes without hesitation. "I'm sorry, but I firmly believe getting married just prior to a forced separation of three long years is extremely unwise. I strongly advise against it."

Sonny and Doris are just two of the countless young people who have to make the agonizing decision of whether or not to marry immediately before an inevitable separation. Sometimes, things work out nicely. Too often, a wrong course of action results in a lifetime of unhappiness.

I hardly ever see any wisdom at all in two people getting married only to be separated by time, oceans and poor communications. Ordinarily, their only reason for saying "I do" is the tremendous fear of losing one another. And essentially, this fear is really indicative of a basic lack of trust and a love that is still shaky, to say the least.

The reasoning, conscious or subconscious, of these couples goes something like this: "If you go away," they think to themselves, "for such a long time, perhaps you will learn to live without me. There is also the distinct possibility that you will meet somebody more attractive than me and because I will be so far away, I will be at such a great disadvantage. Perhaps someone will steal you from me before we are reunited. So, if I marry you now, before you go, I can be sure that 'you are mine, all mine, now and forever' as the song goes."

How true and terrifyingly accurate are these possibilities. I agree with every line … except the last. I strongly doubt that two people, who have hardly lived together as husband and wife and who become separated for two or three years, can be so confident of the solidity of their marriage bond.

Marriage is a tough profession that calls for intense care and round-the-clock vigilance, without which it is hard put to survive. Even the happiest marriage is consistently besieged with all kinds of temptations and problems that need tender loving care.

They say that the first years of married life are the most difficult. How silly to add to the problem by signing a contract which is binding for life just before both parties are forcibly separated by great distances.

I remember the old adage: "Far from sight, far from mind." And I agree fully. What do you do when you wish to forget a person? You walk away and try to sever all modes of communication. If possible, you leave your home and go far away, hoping that time and distance and new friends will erase old memories and hasten the forgetting process.

I prefer to look upon the case of Doris and Sonny as a fine opportunity to test their love. If it is strong and deeply rooted, it will survive the three long years. If something goes wrong and they suddenly find themselves fallen out of love, then they will not have made a fatal mistake which could cause them untold misery.

WHEN A WOMAN HAS A BABY

THIS CHAPTER IS DIRECTED solely at young married men and single males contemplating matrimony.

I am not a doctor. Perhaps it is just as well. I don't have to bother with the physical aspects of having a baby. You might even ask why I care to write anything at all about pregnant women.

Well, the truth of the matter is that, though I feel rather uncomfortable discussing the topic, I find a certain amount of boldness within me that urges me on. Perhaps it is because, in my counseling, I hear so many married women talk about it when complaining about their husbands.

It seems that there are plenty of men who are quite heartless and almost totally lacking in knowledge of the pregnant woman. Without considering the physiological happenings involved, which few men aside from doctors ever really get to understand, there are other factors that need explaining.

First and foremost, is the fact that when a woman is pregnant, her body is undergoing so many physical changes that she very often is not herself. She may be irritable, tired and listless. Don't be surprised if she weeps for no apparent reason.

When a woman is conceiving, she may sometimes give you the impression that she doubts your love for her. I suppose it's because having a baby is no small thing and a woman has to be reassured that the needed emotional security will always be there. So, for God's sake, be more loving than usual. Intensify your exterior manifestations of affection. Spend more evenings at home just being together. There must be absolutely no question of your loyalty and concern for her.

You may think it silly to focus more attention on her this way. Well, we men don't have babies. So, I guess it's difficult for us to understand what it's all about. We males are notorious gripers when it comes to physical discomfort. Women can silently bear a lot more pain than men. So remember, chances are that your wife is suffering more intensely than she cares to tell. Women usually keep most of their pains to themselves because they don't want to "bother or worry" the man they love.

And since a pregnant woman feels uncomfortable most of the time, I can understand (and so do most wives) that a husband cannot forever be at her side. However, there is one crucial moment when a man should definitely stand by his wife, even if it means canceling important engagements.

I am referring to the long hours immediately preceding delivery. The labor pains a woman suffers can only be imagined by us men. I guess we would have to experience them to believe them.

When a woman is in tremendous pain; when she is anxious about her child's and her own physical well-being, she needs the man she loves there at her side or at least in a nearby room to encourage her and to reassure her that everything is going to be alright.

When a couple is having their first baby, the husband is usually a nervous wreck roaming about the corridors like a restless tiger in a cage. And when he finds out that he is the father of a bouncing baby boy or girl, he cannot contain his joy and excitement. He rushes to his wife's bedside, kisses her and wipes her brow, and trips over himself getting her a cold drink of water.

For too many wives, this is a unique once-in-a-lifetime spectacle. After the first child, they no longer see the excited face of their husband when the next child is born. Can you believe that I know of men who were out with the boys—sometimes with the girls—while the poor little wife was giving birth in the hospital?

I think every husband belongs at the side of his wife, whether she is delivering her first or her fifteenth baby. You men may get used to ordering babies, but women never get accustomed to bringing them into the world. I don't think a man can truthfully say that he really loves his wife if he prefers getting a good night's sleep or going out with the gang to being with his woman when her time comes. If he insists that he really loves her but "she can take care of herself," I think he has a terribly warped sense of values.

Someday your wife may come to me with a marital problem. I hope, at least, she may never be able to pronounce this indictment against you: "Bob, can you believe, that when I gave birth he didn't even come to see me until the second day?"

Below is a little prayer I composed after rereading this chapter:

PRAYER OF AN EXPECTANT MOTHER

Lord God, thank you
for this gift of life
that I feel pulsating
within me.
Thank you for my husband
who loves me so dearly
and who respects me so
deeply.
It is our strong mutual love
and your kindness
that have brought into
being
the child that I feel moving
inside me.
Dear Lord, watch over me
during these crucial
months.
Protect me and my baby

from all harm.
I ask not that my delivery
be painless, but
that it be safe for the
fragile life
I am bringing into the
world.
Lord, I offer up to you
my discomfort and,
most especially,
the sufferings I will
experience shortly …

All I ask in return
is that my baby
be born healthy and
happy,
and that it be a living
symbol
of that intense love
my husband and I
have for one another.
Amen.

THE PHONIEST PROOF OF MANHOOD

A MAN'S NATURAL FEELINGS for a woman do not take into account whether she's married or single; of whether she's a friend or a foe; or whether she's virtuous or immoral; or whether he loves her or not.

A body is a body, regardless. Your feelings can't think. When a dog is in heat, there's no stopping her. "It's natural' and she's willing and unashamed. But men are not dogs. And they think—some more than others. And they know that what makes all the difference in the world is the ability of the human mind to say NO to feelings.

This, I believe, marks the measure of maturity in a man. When you were a child, you tried to do just about everything you felt like doing until your parents taught you certain values based on common sense. They showed you how to use the bathroom—even if you didn't feel like it. And to make life more pleasant for everybody, they taught you how to observe certain rules of etiquette—even if you didn't feel like it. And you were urged to share your candies with your kid brothers and sisters—even if you didn't feel like it.

Some people say that it isn't good to repress "natural feelings." I just can't help believing that they are people living on cloud nine (cloud nine is up there somewhere as opposed to good old solid reality down here). Of course, it isn't healthy to repress all your feelings, but to go to the extreme—extremes always run the terrible risk of making you look stupid—and say that you should do "what comes naturally" is utter nonsense.

Think of what would happen if I feel like getting a color TV and I don't have the money; then all I have to do is take it? And if I have a "natural" feeling for that woman, who just happens to be your wife, I should take her whether she likes it or not? Or even if she likes it? It's crazy!

I often hear women say, "Men will be men … so what can you do?" You can help them to grow up, that's what. When I hear women say that, I feel like asking them: "Hey girls, aren't you ever tempted to fool around?" (And I know the answer to that answer to that question too!)

What I'm trying to say is this: sexual intercourse is really no proof of manhood because it's so "naturally" easy. Even idiots do it-and can do it quite well. I think there is more to being a man than having a big body (I'm 6'2" and 210 lbs.) and being able to perform a biological act that is really quite simple.

I believe that manhood can be proven in other, more decisive, ways. On the athletic field and in the classroom, for instance. But most of all, in creative thinking and intense love. I didn't say sex, though sex does have a part to play in love and most of all, in the deep maturing process which eventually enables a man to prove himself the superior being he is by mastering his greatest enemy, which is himself.

What? A guy is a man because he goes to bed with a woman? Easiest thing to do in the whole world. Why, you don't even have to make an effort.

How about saying "no" for a change to that sexy little dish who is more than willing? If you can do it, that we can all start believing you're the man you say you are.

PRAYER OF A MAN WHO CAN'T SAY NO

Lord, help me to keep my head
when the girls start getting too close.
Let me understand that my nature,
which is naturally so strong and wild,
must be harnessed and tamed,
if I am not to make a mess out of my life.
Help me to believe
that it takes more guts to say "no" to that
one hundred pounds of flesh,
than it does to do what comes naturally.
Give me the strength and intelligence
that will enable me
to be the master of myself,
so that I can be the man
I have always longed to be.

THE JEALOUS HUSBAND

AT FIRST, MYRA WAS FLATTERED. Pepito always fussed over her. He drove her to and from work daily. He called the office 2 or 3 times a day to ask about her. He told her what clothes to wear and stayed at home almost every weekend.

Then Myra began to notice a slow change coming over her husband. After five months of marriage, he became increasingly possessive and excessively suspicious. Pepito resented the way she conversed with men—even if they happened to be his wife's relatives.

They quarreled when he accused her of flirting with her friends in the office. Soon he asked her to quit her job and stay at home. When Myra refused, he felt sure that something was going on at work and began going to the office to check on her. Twice he made a scene when he suspected a handsome young clerk of having an affair with his wife.

Within a few months, Myra was no longer flattered. Pepito's irrational jealousy gave rise to countless arguments and created unbearable tension in the house.

Finally, the inevitable happened. After eight months of marriage, Myra left her husband.

Pepito's case is not rare. Jealous husbands abound. You will almost surely find at least one in your family or among your relatives. He is an impossible man to live with. I don't know who is more unbearable, the nagging wife or the jealous husband.

Most people believe that jealousy is a sign of deep love. I'm sorry, I just cannot agree. I hardly think it is a sign of true love. I rather think it is a clear indication of strong distrust. The jealous husband is not sure of his wife. He is convinced that her loyalty is definitely questionable.

The jealous husband or lover is so frightened, so anxious about losing his woman, that he does his utmost to isolate her from any and all males who are potential threats to himself. If she does not mix with men, he reasons, then she will never fall in love with another guy.

Unless he is a very sick man, the jealous husband will not mind if his wife interacts with men he feels do not threaten him. An 80-year old grandfather can talk to her all day and he does not mind, but the moment a good-looking guy says "hi" to his pretty wife, he goes for his gun.

Basically, the jealous husband is a man who is as insecure as he is jealous. In some cases, he may end up in an institution, the victim of a serious mental disorder.

I suppose most men are a little bit jealous of their wives. Perhaps this is because few couples ever achieve complete mutual trust. Or perhaps something in the past has given him legitimate reason to doubt. This is especially true in the case of a woman has had an affair with another man before or after marriage. And, strangely enough, I have found that if a husband has had pre-marital sex with his wife, he very often doubts her ability or willingness to resist other potential lovers.

The jealous husband is a veritable drag on his wife's personal development. Since she remains so restricted in her healthy contacts with people, she does not mature as quickly. And instead of sharing thoughts and experiences with her husband, she is usually hesitant, careful and defensive for fear that he will suspect her of evil doing once again.

What does a woman do about a jealous husband? I guess the trick is to build up his confidence and trust in her. If this does not work, it could be that he is in need of a psychiatrist. At any rate, the poor wife can expect that things will certainly not change overnight.

LOVING IS NOT EASY

THEY SAY THAT "LOVE is a many splendored thing." True. It is also a very confusing and complicated thing.

To begin with, the word "love" is perhaps the most misused and misunderstood word in any language. Everybody throws the word "love" around to describe a multitude of feelings—some having absolutely nothing to do with love.

"I love pancit!" How can you love pancit? You enjoy pancit. You find it delicious. But you cannot love it.

"I loved that movie," or "I loved to travel."

Impossible! A young man once told me: "Bob, last night, I loved a hostess." He did not love the hostess. What he really meant to say was that he had sexual intercourse with her. Besides, this expression, "to make love to a woman" is commonly used whether or not the man loves the woman.

Since the word love is so badly used, we should not be surprised if it is taken very lightly by so many people.

Everybody thinks he is an expert when it comes to love. There is hardly a man who cannot give you his long, drawn out philosophy of loving. And is it not amusing to listen to the playboy (married or single) proudly talk about his countless "love" affairs? Whenever I hear a man boasting about his innumerable sexual conquests and passing them off as "love" affairs, I feel I am witnessing a tragic comedy.

They say it is natural to love. I agree. People almost unanimously believe that it is easy to "fall in love." I say, amen!

However, what many men and women fail to realize is that loving is not simply falling in love. "Falling" in love is easy. Most often, you do not have to try. You just "fall." but to make love grow in depth and intensity is something else again.

Look around in your families and among your friends and you will discover how often people fail in love. See those houses that are not homes; those couples who continue to live together "for the sake of the children"; the legions of separated men and women and the broken homes they have left behind; notice the gaudy nightclubs crowded with unhappy husbands. All this bears witness to the fact that loving truly and deeply is not as easy as it sounds .... that it remains one of the toughest challenges of man.

In this marvelous space age, when we have sent men to the moon and find ourselves reaching for the stars, isn't it strange that we are still backward in our knowledge and application of fraternal and marital love? Indeed, many believe that we are losing ground and, as they watch the "break-up" of our society, they feel we are forgetting the "true sense" of love.

At any rate, I think that all of you who have tried unsuccessfully to experience deep and meaningful love will agree with me when I say that loving isn't easy. And I am equally confident that those readers among you who are happily in love will not argue with me when I say: "To make love grow and to keep it strong and healthy, is a 24-hour a day job."

FIGHT, YES, BUT FIGHT CLEAN

THERE IS HARDLY ANY COUPLE that doesn't, at one time or another, fight. Not only couples, but even just plain and simple friends have it out on occasion.

Whenever I do counseling, I very often resort to fighting to settle things. What I do is bring the troubled people together and then I do everything in my power to encourage everybody to blow off steam. Most of the time, this almost surely means that fighting will break out. But I don't really mind. In fact, the trouble with many people is that they find difficulty in expressing their negative thoughts and feelings about others.

Fighting, if it is productive, has a way of straightening many crooked ideas. And if people only knew how to fight fairly and constructively, the result would be well worthwhile and quite fascinating. The problem lies in the fact that most people "fight dirty" and the results are often negative and destructive.

I think that timing is of utmost importance in productive fighting. Some people almost pick the wrong time to argue. It isn't time to start fighting when a man is just about ready to leave the house for work, or when he is flat on his back in a hospital bed.

The best time to start a productive fight is when both parties are as rested and as unemotional as possible.

The second point to remember is to keep your fighting confined to current issues. Stay away from ancient history. Lots of people fight dirty. The husband talks about his wife's former boyfriend (that was 38 years ago); the wife brings out an old argument that she had with her in-laws 10 years ago in which he sided with his mother.

If there is to be a constructive fight that will bring about positive results, the multitude of past hurts have to be left out for the moment. Besides, more often than not, these old skeletons are usually brought forth to simply hurt or to draw attention away from the issue at hand.

A third point to remember is to agree on what you are fighting about. How many times have I listened to two people arguing about different things and not get together? When a woman says she is angry at her husband for coming home late after office, is it the hours he keeps, or is it that she suspects that there is another woman? And when a husband fights with his wife about the length of her skirt, is it really the hemline or is it that he doesn't trust her?

The fourth rule to remember is always to be frank and open. Reality is hard enough to deal with without throwing up a smoke screen of lies and fantasies. Nothing productive will ever come from a fight if the truth is hidden away beneath layers of pride, deceit and dishonesty.

Finally, and perhaps most important of all: NEVER, NEVER TRY TO WIN A FIGHT. Many wives have won countless arguments and lost their husbands. If you must win, then your loved one must have to lose. If your love is to grow, nobody must lose. Both parties must somehow come to a better understanding of the problem so that the cause of the discord can be worked at by all concerned.

Fighting can be productive, educational, and certainly interesting if you fight openly and honestly, concentrate on the here and now, and always strive to find a way out.

TWO DIFFERENT WAYS OF LOVING

A PSYCHOLOGIST ONCE COMPARED married life to the stage: "Love for the woman is itself the drama; for the man, it is the intermission."

For the man, love is a very powerful impulse, very sexual in nature. It forms only part of his sphere of interest. In other words, a man feels that there is more to life than loving. There is his work, sports, politics and the creative arts. There is the challenge and adventure of competition.

On the other hand, love, for a woman, continues a whole way of life. It is not a part time activity for her. Everything she does, she does out of love. Otherwise, her life becomes stained with bitterness. A woman looks at love as something that is all-encompassing and all-embracing.

For her, love means a permanent high level of affection. Loving becomes almost an obsession. There is no need to call for a "time out." in fact, she stands in mortal fear of ever having to experience a decline in the affection she receives from her loved one.

This is why a wife always longs to be with her husband and wants to know all about his work—even though she understands little or nothing about it. And when her husband does not want to talk about it because he is aware that it is beyond her and not because he no longer loves her, she gets hurt and begins to suspect something is drastically wrong with her marriage. She cannot understand that her husband does not care to talk just for the sake of talking. He cannot comprehend the fact that it is not understanding his work that is so important to his wife; it is more the TIME and the ATTENTION that he gives her.

A woman counts the hours a man spends with her. The man places more importance on what is put into those hours. A woman needs to hear tender words from the man she loves. She has to FEEL and CONSTANTLY remain secure. Although a man needs to feel his woman's love also, he is more readily satisfied with KNOWING his wife/sweetheart loves him. His need to FEEL and to be continuously reassured is not as deep as his female counterpart.

If her husband goes off to watch a basketball game without her, the wife may get hurt unnecessarily. If he shows interest in other things, it is not because he is no longer interested in her. In fact, the man loves her deeply. However, doing EVERYTHING together does not come into his concept of love. He believes he can still love his wife and care very much for other matters. In other words, his wife is not everything to him.

The different concepts of love create confusion and sometimes wreak havoc in marriages and courtships. It often happens that we witness the tragic spectacle of two people madly in love wildly battling each other because of lack of understanding of the basic differences in the male and female concept of loving. It is not that the woman's way of loving is better. Nor is it a question of who is right and who is wrong. The truth lies in the fact that both concepts are simply different. Once a couple understands this and *accepts* it, you can be sure that they will avoid the many traps and pitfalls that less mature couples inevitably fall into.

About the Author

Bob Garon was born in New Hampshire USA. He was sent to the Philippines in 1965 to do missionary work. He left the priesthood and received his dispensation from his vows in 1978. By being involved in organizations that addressed the needs of troubled youth, Bob built a name for himself and is known as the Father of the Therapeutic Community in Asia.

As a writer and columnist, he has written over 14,000 articles over the past four decades. He has helped and inspired countless individuals and couples through his live phone-in counseling on radio and television, as well as with motivational speaking.

Bob also set-up a management consultancy firm, and, together with his wife Emmy, founded the Golden Values Schools.

Up to his last days, Bob worked with people struggling to overcome various addictions and helped them get their lives back together. He passed away in 2021 at the age of 85.

Thank you for reading!

If you received value from this book, please consider leaving a review, however short, on the Amazon page. This will help get the message to others who may need or appreciate it.

Royalties earned from this book will help poor children in the Philippines get an education.

* * *

OTHER BOOKS WRITTEN BY BOB GARON

Facing Life's Problems
Love & Courtship
The Challenge of Marriage

Made in the USA
Columbia, SC
26 November 2024

47103931R00119